M000277901

The Three-Day
Feast

Maundy Thursday, Good Friday, Easter

Gail Ramshaw

Augsburg Fortress

THE THREE-DAY FEAST
Maundy Thursday, Good Friday, Easter

Editors: Suzanne Burke, Jessica Hillstrom
Cover and interior design: Laurie Ingram
Cover photo: Nicolas Russell/Getty Images

ISBN 0-8066-5115-6

Manufactured in the U.S.A.

07   06   05   04   1   2   3   4   5   6   7   8   9   10

This book is dedicated to the memory of Alexander Schmemann,

who in 1970 tutored its author in the meaning of the liturgies of Easter.

Contents

Introduction

Many Christians are already familiar with the ancient, and now recently restored, liturgies of the Three Days: Maundy Thursday, Good Friday, and the great Easter Vigil service of light, readings, baptism, and communion. The worship resources published by the Evangelical Lutheran Church in America, the Episcopal Church, the United Methodist Church, the Presbyterian Church U.S.A. and the Roman Catholic Church all include nearly identical versions of these liturgies. During these past decades one assembly after another has revived these rites and found in them unexpected riches, an astonishing feast each year. Some of the faithful have come to treasure these Three Days as the heart of their worship life and the grounding of their spirituality, and some young people have participated in these services annually since they were toddlers. Yet other Christians have never used these liturgies, and perhaps have not even heard much about them. This book is crafted with the hope that both those who are newly experiencing these services and those for whom the liturgies are already beloved will be drawn deeper into the meaning of the Three Days and closer to all other Christians who celebrate the Resurrection of Our Lord in this way.

Welcome to the three-day feast.

1
Keeping a Feast

In the English language, one interesting use of the verb "to keep" is found in the title of this chapter: we keep a feast. We can say that we mark the solstice, we celebrate Thanksgiving, we remember the date of our baptism, we observe the anniversary of a death, we hold a birthday party. But also we can say that we keep holidays, anniversaries, and birthdays.

There is deep truth in this use of "keep." To keep is to retain something, to hold it close, to preserve it, to protect it. Festivals need to be "kept," or their influence over our lives will cease. Because our lives are so complicated, our energies spent on so many necessities, with new interests daily competing for our attention, we must intentionally strive to keep alive remembrance of what we choose to value. If we do not keep, in our minds and hearts, our son-in-law's birthday or our grandmother's deathday, these events will fade away, and their importance will be lost to us.

Anniversaries and holidays are not only reminders of value for the individual self, but they work as memory glue for the community. So it is that since the beginnings of human communities, people have kept such events with others, by gathering for a festive meal, dressing in fancy clothes, sending greetings, or giving presents. We keep the feast, not only within our own consciousness, but with the assembled community. One of the primary ways that one human society is distinguished from another is in the festivals it keeps, and one of the fundamental issues for an interreligious marriage is how to keep which celebrations.

If we keep the feast, the feast will keep us. Its values will remain in the community, its ideals will inspire us, and its spirit of comfort and hope will help to sustain us. Even if the "feast" that we keep is as basic as the family dinner, that regular gathering will work to shape the family members into a community of collaboration and conversation.

Perhaps at our family dinner on January 6 we sing a Christmas carol about the magi's visit to the baby Jesus, but perhaps we keep the festival of Epiphany in a bigger way, by holding an annual house blessing. Gathering outside the front door of the house, some Christian families mark the doorframe of their home with the year's date and the letters C, M, and B. The letters stand for Caspar, Melchior, and Balthasar (the names that tradition has given to the magi), and also for the Latin phrase meaning "Christ, bless this house" (for the M, think "mansion"). The family has kept Epiphany, and throughout the year the chalk markings will keep alive their prayer for God's blessing.

Telling the story

One of the primary methods that communities use when keeping a commemoration is to tell the story. The elders gather the community around and pour out their hearts, along with their memories, so that the youths will know what to value. The sagas are sung, the bedtime stories are read, the obituary is heard. Those marrying into a family must listen to all the family tales, whether or not the stories are even remotely accurate! To learn about people of another culture, we first listen to the stories of their past. Annually on the Fourth of July, the

New York Times prints a full-page facsimile of the Declaration of Independence, and at least some of us read at least part of it each year. Some Americans begin their Thanksgiving dinner by reading from the diaries of the pilgrims the description of their first harvest festival. The past events are kept in mind over the centuries only because the story is told over and over again. To remember the event, we tell the story.

The opening verses of the book of Luke describe to us this method of remembrance. By the time Luke wrote, the eyewitnesses to the ministry of Jesus were dying off. A first generation had already written accounts of the life of Jesus, but Luke hopes to tell the story in a more complete way and with more focused meaning. Over the first century many gospels were written so that later Christians would hear the story told, and second-century church leaders chose the four in our Bibles as the ones that they judged told the story most faithfully. Because we Christians need to hold Jesus in our memory, we assemble weekly to hear the story. In many churches, the entire assembly stands during the proclamation of the gospel, acknowledging that the voice of Christ is actually speaking in this room, on this day, in this reading.

Over the centuries, Christians developed various devotional services that told the story of the suffering and death of Christ. One well-known practice is built around the Stations of the Cross. Roman Catholic churches depict the Stations of the Cross in art on their walls. Recently some Protestant churches have crafted Lenten services based on these Stations. With prayers and meditations, these devotions trace what are usually fourteen biblical and nonbiblical stops along Christ's road of suffering and death. The ritual was developed and popularized by the Franciscan friars during the fourteenth century. They sought to bring to each parish a copy of what the Crusaders had established in Jerusalem, a walk through the retelling of the passion of Christ.

A second Lenten devotion, the Seven Last Words, is similarly a retelling of the story. The pattern was invented in 1687 by Alonso Messia, a Jesuit priest in Peru. If the four gospels are combined together, Jesus is remembered as speaking seven times from the cross. Also called the Devotion of the Three Hours, this practice gathers the assembly on Good Friday for the three hours that Jesus was on the cross. The assembly listens to sermons based on these "seven last words" and sings appropriate hymns, such as the seven-part "Jesus, in thy dying woes." In some communities, this service is ecumenical, with preachers of different Christian denominations each taking a turn for the sermons.

A third Lenten devotion called Tenebrae developed out of the morning prayers of monastic communities during medieval times. Now usually held on one of the evenings of Holy Week, Tenebrae retells the story of the death of Christ by reading the long passion narrative in short sections and interspersing the readings with prayers from the biblical Book of Lamentations. After each section one of a number of candles is extinguished. Various usages suggest different numbers of candles and the treatment and significance of the last candle. At the conclusion of the narrative, some kind of loud crash is produced, which in the darkened church scares people to death. However, the point of the devotion is to tell the story of Christ.

In each of these examples we see a practice not much different from prehistoric tribes gathered around a bonfire to listen to the poets chanting about their heroes. Our communal story is part of our identity, and we need each year to hear our significant stories. It is as if each part of our story is a vertebra of our backbone, a foundation stone for our castle. Without a spinal column, without a foundation, we totter and sink.

Enacting the meaning

The second method that communities use when keeping a commemoration is to enact its meaning. Most Americans do not reread the Declaration of Independence annually on the Fourth of July. Instead, they enact the meaning of the day. They revel in freedom by taking a vacation day, attending a picnic, watching fireworks. Their activities proclaim the significance of the day: not their words, but their actions say that today we are free. Neither do most Americans begin their Thanksgiving dinner by reading the pilgrims' accounts. Instead, they enact the meaning of the occasion by gathering with family and friends, beginning the meal with prayer, eating a surfeit of traditional foods and, just like the pilgrims and the Native Americans, staging sporting events. Without retelling the story, they act out its meaning.

The first chapter of Genesis describes a ritual of enacted meaning. The ancient tale says that God created the world in six days and rested on the seventh. Jews "keep" the meaning of God's order in their lives by mimicking the actions of the creator. So they rest on the seventh day. It is interesting that in Deuteronomy 5, the Sabbath is given a different meaning: the weekly freedom from work recalls the Israelites' freedom from slavery in Egypt. With either explanation, the Jewish keeping of the weekly Sabbath enacts a primary belief for the people. The Jews live out the meaning of creation and the Exodus by how they conduct themselves on Saturdays.

We see a clear example of enacted meaning in the ritual of Ash Wednesday. For this day of the Christian calendar, no biblical account about Jesus and ashes that we can read aloud provides the actual story. The readings appointed for Ash Wednesday do not even include one of the several Old Testament descriptions of ancient peoples sitting in ashes or pouring ashes on their head. Yet an increasing number of Protestants around the world are joining with Roman Catholics in the centuries-old practice of receiving a cross of ashes on their forehead. The ashes "say" the meaning of the day. We begin the

Lenten forty days by acknowledging that we are mortal and will die, that we lament our sins, and that we need to be washed with baptismal waters. We keep Ash Wednesday with an action, and perhaps here the dictum applies, that actions speak louder than words.

We are all far more aware than we used to be about the power of actions to form values and shape minds. The education of children is achieved not only by years of reading and hours of storytelling. Rather, by attending interactive museums, creating art, building models, participating in pageants and other such activities, children plant their learning into their psyches more firmly than they would by listening to someone else talk. If we hope to rear our children as Christians, we cannot only talk to them of Christ. We need to find ways for them to join with us to enact the meaning of Christ.

Both story and meaning

Christians keep the Sunday that begins Holy Week with a service that includes both story and action. For the palm procession on the Sunday of the Passion (sometimes called Palm Sunday), we read the story of Jesus' entry into Jerusalem from Matthew, Mark, or Luke. Following the reading, the palms are blessed and the assembly processes into the church, waving its palms. Many assemblies sing the traditional hymn "All glory, laud, and honor," which legend says was written on this feast day in the year 821 by an imprisoned bishop, Theodulph of Orleans, while the palm procession passed by his jail. Walking into the church with our palms readies us for our own experience of Jerusalem, which continues with the full reading of the passion account from Matthew, Mark, or Luke. During the sermon, perhaps the children play at constructing a cross out of their palm frond. So it is that on Passion/Palm Sunday, we do both: we tell the story and enact its meaning.

A famous example of how Christians both told the story and enacted its meaning is found in a remarkable diary kept by a woman named Egeria who in about the year 400 was on pilgrimage in the Holy Land during Holy Week. She recorded details of the services held at the places revered because of their connection to the death and resurrection of Christ. At each location on each day, the appropriate scriptural passages that told the story of Jesus were read out to the assembly, and then various rituals were conducted so the people could enact the meaning of the text with their very bodies.

Particularly interesting is her description of the Good Friday rites. About 80 years prior, Emperor Constantine's mother, Helena, had excavated at Golgotha what she believed was Christ's true cross, and on Good Friday this cross was set up for veneration by the faithful. Egeria writes:

> The bishop grips the ends of the sacred wood with his hands, while the deacons, who are standing about, keep watch over it. There is a reason why it is guarded in this manner. It is the practice here for all the people to come forth one by one, the faithful as well as the catechumens, to bow down before the table, kiss the holy wood, and then move on. It is said that someone (I do not know when) took a bite and stole a piece of the holy cross. Therefore, it is now guarded by the deacons standing around, lest there be anyone who would dare come and do that again.[1]

The passion narrative was read from the gospels, and then the people processed forward to reverence what was called the "True Cross." Here was the combination of both listening and doing, both story and activity.

Perhaps the most effective "keeping" occurs in such combining. It may well be that hearing a story is easier than doing its meaning. Listening to the gospel narration of Jesus' entry into Jerusalem is surely less complicated than also purchasing palms, getting them into people's hands, organizing the procession, figuring out how the singing will work while people are walking around, and deciding what to do if it's pouring rain. Yet by doing the procession, we enter into the biblical narrative with our very bodies, and we join with countless Christians who for many centuries have paraded on this Sunday, singing their hosannas to the crucified and risen Christ. Participating in the palm procession brings more than our ears into the worship. The hope is that our actions in the liturgy become a first sign that our entire lives mean to enact the meaning of the day's readings. First we hear, then we act: first in the liturgy, then with our lives.

A Prayer~

O God, you are our Keeper,
protecting us all the day long,
embracing us through the night.
Keep all the world in your mercy,
and enable us to keep and share your Spirit
through Jesus Christ, our Savior and Lord.
Amen.

For reflection and discussion

1. What were some holidays significant in the lives of your parents and grandparents that you no longer keep? Are you glad or sad to drop them?
2. Kwanzaa, the African-American observance at the close of December, was invented by a university professor in 1972. How does it function in your community?
3. What is good, and what is problematic, about keeping anniversaries of tragedies, such as 9/11?
4. Have you any stories to tell about how your family tells stories?
5. Cite examples from elementary schools of children learning by doing.

2
Keeping the Resurrection of Our Lord

Patterns for Easter

For Christians, the annual festival of supreme value is what English speakers call Easter. Although anyone who studies history knows that in the first century a Jewish man named Jesus (in Aramaic, Yeshuah) was executed by Rome, what makes people Christians is the community's faith in him as the incarnation of God and their resurrected Savior. Easter identifies Christians for what they are: the body of this risen Lord. Christians keep Easter in a big way because the death and resurrection of Christ keeps them. The death and resurrection of Christ keeps us sustained by the mercy of God, accompanied by the throngs of the baptized and open to the needs of the world.

Christians have developed many different ways to keep this annual event. We begin our tour with the voluminous journals of Henry Melchior Muhlenberg. Pastor Muhlenberg was the German immigrant who served as a sort of bishop to the many Lutheran communities in the Philadelphia area during the decades before and during the American Revolution. Over the 45 years of his ministry, even he kept Holy Week and Easter in quite different ways. At their fullest, for example in 1765, the days included a preaching service and the two-hour questioning of those preparing for confirmation on Maundy Thursday; a preaching service and confirmation on Good Friday; a second preaching service in the afternoon of Good Friday; registration for communion and private confessions on Holy Saturday; a service with communion for hundreds on Easter Sunday morning; the baptisms of several children, one child's funeral, and a second service on Easter Sunday afternoon; and a third service in the evening. Yet in 1787, the last year of his life, Muhlenberg wrote, "April 8, Easter Sunday. No public worship here today. We two old people had domestic devotions."[2]

Most years, however, Muhlenberg reports large numbers of Lutherans hearing the word and celebrating communion on Easter Day. Yet in some midwestern Lutheran communities in the early twentieth century, the Easter service was only a preaching service, while a totally penitential, even lugubrious, communion service was scheduled for Good Friday. The men, who sat on the right side of the church, communed first, and the women, who sat with the children on the left side of the church, communed second. In many Midwestern towns, only one meal was eaten on Good Friday: home-made noodles and stewed prunes.

Far from these practices are those of the contemporary Yaqui Indians. Two groups of these Native American Christians who live near Tucson, Arizona, find Easter so significant for their identity that they have named their villages Pascua, from the Spanish word for Easter. On each of the Fridays of Lent, the Yaqui communities gather for a ritual that combines Christian medieval penitential rites with their own traditional tribal springtime ceremonies. Prehistorically these tribes were hunters who relied on the deer herds, and so their ancient religious rituals included dances that expressed their admiration for and gratitude to the deer. In their current practice, the culminating Easter pageants blend together a passion play and the burning of Judas in effigy with both a winding of the Maypole and their annual Deer Dance. Throughout Lent, all over the reservation, images of the Deer Dancer have been covered over, and on Easter Day, the Yaquis remove the coverings, as if in the retelling of the story of Christ's resurrection, the Deer Dancer celebrates the return of life to the people.[3]

Today the Pennsylvania Amish hold no community worship on Maundy Thursday or Good Friday, although the people fast until noon on Good Friday and spend the afternoon visiting family and friends. Among the Old Order Amish, who do not build houses of worship, Sunday services are conducted only every other week, with each family taking a turn to host the German service in its home. So Easter Sunday may, or may not, be a day of communal worship. If it is, the service includes one of the two annual observances of communion, and so it will last from eight in the morning until four in the afternoon. The rite of Holy Communion always includes a footwashing—men washing the feet of men and women of women—and the slow a cappella singing of many stanzas of hymns from their 1583 hymnal. Even though it is Easter, the mood will be extremely somber: "They really stress the crucifixion," said an Amish-Mennonite woman from Lancaster, Pennsylvania.[4] Family festivities are held on Easter Monday, along with a traditional Pennsylvania German dinner. The adults give the children chocolates, and the children give the adults flowers.

The Easter service of the Russian Orthodox Christians who gather north of New York City begins early on Saturday evening and lasts throughout the night. By dawn the service is finally over and the communal Easter breakfast begins, with everyone enjoying all the sweet and rich foods that they have fasted from during Lent. Some Protestants keep the feast with a congregational Easter breakfast, although they probably did not observe any Lenten fast. In past decades Easter sunrise services were held at outdoor movie theaters, with each carload of people more or less able to sing with joy and gusto the appointed Easter hymns.

Perhaps you know of other Christian patterns of Easter observance. Thinking through these diverse practices, we can judge that some are more profound, more celebratory, more engrossing, more enlivening, more sustaining, than are others. Some tell the story and enact its meaning more fully than do others. Because many worship leaders are now urging us to restore the early church rites of Maundy Thursday, Good Friday, and the Vigil of Easter, let us now consider these rites and how they came into being.

From equinox to Easter

In many places around the world, prehistoric peoples paid close attention to the sun. Without the sun, life on earth would cease, and realizing this, communities gathered for great festivals at the summer and winter solstices and the spring and autumn equinoxes. It was as if the people needed to cheer the sun on its way, and especially at the equinoxes, to celebrate the perfect balance of day and night, light and darkness. If the universe is in balance, so might the people be.

We know that many herding societies practiced a springtime ritual in which either the first lamb born to the flock or a yearling was sacrificed to the deities. When the people conducted the ritual of a burnt offering, it was as if the death of the lamb could ensure the life of the people. Perhaps everyone knows, deep down, that there is no life without death, no birth without pain, no meal without the sacrifice of animals or plants. Many ancient peoples conducted some kind of ritual that enacted the realization that for us to survive, blood must be shed. In some locales, spring equinox became the time for this sacrifice of the lamb, by which the people pleaded for both the life of the cosmos and the food on their tables.

In agricultural societies, the ripening of the first grain in the springtime became the occasion for communal festivities. We read in the Bible that for a week, only bread baked from the new barley was eaten, and no leaven left over from the previous year was used. The newly harvested food symbolized the newness of the year.

Sometime around 1250 B.C., the people we know as the Israelites added a layer of meaning to their springtime festivals. At the occasion of the first full moon after the spring equinox—this timing meant that even more of the cosmos was in balance—the people sacrificed a lamb and ate unleavened bread, calling this combined festival *Pesach*, which is Hebrew for *Pascha*, Passover. The main point of this festival was to keep alive the memory of their most significant historical event: the exodus from Egypt and their safe passage through the Red Sea. In this event the people had been passed over by the angel of death when God punished their oppressors. The people had been saved, not only from an endless winter or barren fields, but from slavery to the Egyptians. Thanks to the mercy of God, the sun sustained them, the flocks had multiplied, the crops flourished, and their time of servitude had ended.

During the lifetime of Jesus, Pesach was the most important religious holiday for Jews. The gospels report that Jesus kept Passover by making pilgrimage to Jerusalem. It was at Pascha that, Jesus being in Jerusalem, he was arrested, tried, and executed. How could the followers of the Messiah make sense of his death? As Paul writes in 1 Corinthians 5:7-8, "Our paschal lamb, Christ, has been sacrificed. Therefore, let us celebrate the festival." In this way, Christians added yet another layer of meaning to the the ancient rite of springtime.

John the Baptist is remembered as having called Jesus the Lamb of God. Much of the language that Christians use to describe the benefits of the cross—we are redeemed, rescued, saved—derives originally from Jewish vocabulary praising God for the exodus. A famous sermon preached in the second century by Melito, the bishop of a city in present-day Turkey, says it this way:

> "I am the one," says the Christ.
> "I am your forgiveness,
> I am the Pascha of salvation,

> I am the lamb slain for you;
> I am your light,
> I am your resurrection." [5]

Like the lambs of old, Christ was slain. His blood marks our door and protects us from the angel of death. Justin, a second-century layman, likened Jesus' cross to the double spit, one stick horizontal and one vertical, on which the lamb was roasted.

Like the food of the lamb, Christ's body sustains us, not only annually, but in the meal we hold Sunday after Sunday. Like the newly harvested grain, Christ has given us life, not only this year, not only at our meals, but into eternity. The death and resurrection of Christ became for Christians what the Exodus is for the Jews, that is, the past event most determinative of the community's present and future. On top of the springtime celebration of balance in the universe, the blessing of the herds, the new year's food, and the release from slavery, Christians have added their own focus. We celebrate the life granted to the community through the forgiveness granted by God.

Historians are not sure for how many decades early Christians continued to keep the Jewish Pascha. But we know that by the second century, debates arose as to precisely when Christians ought to keep what was now their annual feast. One group maintained that, as Pascha, it ought to stay on the first full moon after the spring equinox, but others asserted that it is always on Sunday that Christians celebrate the resurrection. Sunday won. So for Christians, our springtime festival of life is kept on the first Sunday after the first full moon after the spring equinox. Because there are both an ancient way and a modern way to calculate the spring equinox, Eastern Orthodox Christians compute this date differently than Protestants and Roman Catholics, but all give the same explanation for what they are doing.

Nearly all Christians in every world language, except English speakers, call this festival "Pascha." Oddly, English speakers call the Resurrection of Our Lord "Easter," a word derived from the name of an Anglo-Saxon goddess of dawn (think of the word *east*). Some Christians who speak English think that we should change our practice and join with others to call this festival Pascha, and so keep in remembrance that this is our celebration of Passover.

It is by juxtaposing the death of the Savior with the life of the people that the deepest religious truth can be found. Easter cannot be only about flowers, for human communities of every millennium have been wise enough to ask the question: what died, that these flowers may live? So by the time of the fourth century, Christians spread out their keeping of Pascha over the Three Days in order to express more fully the truth of Christ's death and resurrection and its meaning for the world. Services were held on Maundy Thursday and Good Friday, culminating in the great Vigil of Easter. The liturgies of the Three Days were understood as being one single event that both told the story and enacted its meaning.

Early Christians believed that the most appropriate way for the community to enact the resurrection was to schedule most of its baptisms at the Easter Vigil. In Romans 6, Paul writes of our baptism as our entry into the death and resurrection of Christ, and so baptisms, along with the renewal of baptismal vows, become an obvious—even logically necessary—part of how the assembly enacts Easter. Ambrose, the fourth-century bishop of Milan who baptized Augustine at the Easter Vigil in A.D. 387, describes baptism as our Passover, our passing from death to life. As the poet Susan Palo Cherwien writes,

> Grand juncture of dying and living
> A drowning deep blue into newness
> Embracing Christ's death and arising
> Blest cross, sign anointing our forehead. [6]

Baptism means to reorient our lives, from the crib to the grave, by the light of Christ. The liturgies of the Three Days suggest that we will grasp more fully the meaning of baptism if we hold it next to the empty tomb.

For Christians living in the Northern Hemisphere, it is fortunate that the three-day feast occurs in the springtime. All of nature appears to be coming to life, and the influential theologians whom we call "the church fathers" made much of this symbolism in their Easter sermons. Some preachers also tied Easter to Christmas by computing the nine months between the two festivals and thus claiming that Jesus was conceived in Mary's womb at Pascha. Not only what is natural, but also what is supernatural begins anew at this time.

The Three Days, lost and found again

The centuries brought many cultural changes. It came to be that Christians baptized infants at birth, and so the Easter Vigil was no longer a gathering of the whole community for adult baptisms. After the fourth century, with European countries becoming nominally Christian, celebrating that religious identity became less important in people's lives. Monks and nuns residing in monasteries and convents took over the elaborate liturgies of the church, with far simpler services provided for lay people in the churches, led by sometimes poorly educated clergy. Many clergy mistranslated the word Pascha, thinking that it referred not to the Passover, but to Christ's passion. In consequence, the church focused more and more on Christ's suffering and popularized devotions that emphasized only the crucifixion. At the time of the sixteenth-century Reformation, its leaders, for example Martin Luther and John Calvin, knew less about the early church's keeping of the Three Days than you as a reader of this book now know, and so Protestants at that time did not revive these rites. Unaware of the pattern of the Easter Vigil, Moravians invented the Easter sunrise service, which spread to other Protestant churches.

The seventeenth century witnessed a momentous alteration of Protestant and Roman Catholic church buildings: pews were installed. Before that time, churches had benches or stools here and there, but no permanent and ordered seating that lined people up as if each person was a word on a printed page. In the recent film *Luther*, one scene depicts a church service. As he preaches, Luther is walking up and down the aisle, while the people are seated in high-backed pews. Both depictions are inaccurate: Luther would have stood in the pulpit to preach, indeed the only way that all the people, who would have been standing around or sitting on the floor, would have been able to see and hear him.

The fact that churches have permanent seating in rows has convinced many people that worship is sitting quietly in your place while somebody else reads to you. Some churches maintain the practice of passing out communion to the people, so that they can remain sitting in their pews. For those congregations that still imagine worship in this way, the procession with palms on Passion Sunday, as well as many of the actions in the liturgies of the Three Days, may seem out of place. Indeed, nearly every action is "out of place" if your place is sitting quietly in your pew. Chairs in straight rows may be good for listening to a story, but they may pose an obstacle when we try to enact the meaning of the story.

Midway in the twentieth century, because of increasing religious pluralism and a weakening of governmental support for Christianity, sociologists noted that the emerging situation of the church was more like that of the fourth century than of the thirteenth or the sixteenth, and so liturgical reformers suggested that we could learn something from early church worship patterns. People began to think again about the usefulness—indeed, the grandeur—of the way that earlier Christians kept Holy Week, and many educators and liturgists spoke about the effectiveness of enacting what we hear. Worship offices began to publish versions of these Holy Week services, which some people called by their Latin name, the Triduum, and others, preferring vernacular English, entitled the Three Days. Many people who participated in these services came to love them and urged others to keep Easter in this way. The 1978 *Lutheran Book of Worship* included these rites, but only in the Ministers Desk Edition, and so some lay people never knew these service orders existed. A revision of these Lutheran services is now available in *The Church's Year,* Renewing Worship, vol. 8 (Minneapolis: Augsburg Fortress, 2004), with the hope that each year more congregations will celebrate Maundy Thursday, Good Friday, and the Resurrection of Our Lord in this way.

We might well inquire why these days are called Three, since by usual counting, Thursday through Sunday would be four. Religious stories are filled with three-day-long events. We count Maundy Thursday as one, Good Friday as two, and, recalling that in biblical times a day was said to begin at sundown the night before, Saturday evening as the start of day three. So it is that many Christians keep the Three Days with the ancient services of Maundy Thursday, Good Friday, and the Vigil of Easter Eve, as well as with the more familiar Easter morning celebration.

One pastoral issue continuing in the twenty-first century is that throngs of people attend a celebratory service on Easter Day without having kept in any way an observance of the passion and death of Christ. Indeed, the phrase "Easter Christians" refers to those countless of the baptized who attend worship only once a year, on Easter. The medieval church officials talked about one's "Easter duty": each baptized Christian must go to church at least on Easter in order to be considered a Christian and avoid excommunication. The truth here is that keeping Easter is the single most significant identity-marker for Christians.

Yet for those church members who worship only on Easter, if the Easter service is all joyous music, rented trumpeters, banks of flowers, pretty hats, and egg hunts for the children, Christian identity has shrunk to only a small part of its meaning. The seriousness of this shrinkage is one impetus to the contemporary movement to revive in our time the ancient pattern of keeping the Easter experience. Since

the death of Christ has meaning for Christians only because of the resurrection, and since the resurrection has no weight without attention
to Jesus' suffering and death, it is wise to understand the Three Days
as one single feast, three days long. We journey together through the
feast, beginning on Maundy Thursday, including Good Friday, culminating at the Vigil of Easter, and continuing through Easter Day.

A hymn written by Susan Briehl says the Easter faith in this way:

> Holy God, holy and beautiful,
> beauty unsurpassed,
> you are despised, rejected;
> scorned, you hold us fast,
> and we behold your beauty.
>
> Holy God, holy and living one,
> life that never ends,
> you show your love by dying,
> dying for your friends,
> and we behold you living. [7]

The words of the stanzas weave into one cloth what we might first
think of as opposite strands: the holy God and the crucified Jesus,
beauty and suffering, life and death. The rites of the Three Days proclaim this same marriage of opposites. The Holy Communion of
Maundy Thursday, the devotion of Good Friday, and the celebrations
of Easter need one another for each to have its most profound
Christian truth. The Three Days do not mean for us to pretend that
we are back in approximately A.D. 35, walking around with Jesus.
Rather, we keep all three days inspired by the Spirit of the resurrection. We commemorate the process from death to life, but throughout all the worship services, we are Easter people.

Of course Christians find it familiar that we need three to say one.
In speaking of God, we are different from our Jewish and Muslim
cousins, for Christians affirm that the one God is known in three and

that the Father, Son, and Holy Spirit are co-equal. To know the Creator, we need to know also the Savior and the Advocate. To praise the Majesty, we receive the Word and embody the Spirit. One is flat without its three dimensions. We can say the same for Easter: to be embraced by Easter, we need also to embrace Maundy Thursday and Good Friday.

A Prayer~

O God, you are our Passover,
marking our doors against danger,
providing the food for our journey.
Open for us all
a way to safety and the path to new life
through Jesus Christ, our Savior and Lord.
Amen.

For reflection and discussion

1. Should English speakers join the rest of the Christian world by calling this festival Pascha?
2. If instead of being yourself, you were either Yaqui or Amish, which would you choose?
3. What is your favorite part of how your assembly observes Holy Week? What is your least favorite part? Why?
4. How do you observe Holy Week and Easter in your homes?
5. What would be better about Sunday worship if our buildings had no seating?
6. Ought Christians in the Southern Hemisphere keep Easter during their springtime, which is autumn for North Americans?

3
The Three Days:
Maundy Thursday

The body of Christ

On Maundy Thursday, the first of the Three Days, the church partici-
pates in one of the constants of human life: marking significant occa-
sions with a meal. Since ancient times, when people establish a new
relationship, they conclude the covenant event with a meal. Rites of
passage such as birthday parties, weddings, housewarmings, and
funerals are accompanied with food. Many wedding receptions
include the ritual of the groom and bride feeding one another.
Oftentimes even a casual meeting between adult friends calls for a
cup of coffee. It seems that eating together bonds people into one.
The one table makes the assembled people one. Food enlivens the
body—both one's own body and the body of the community.

The Bible tells many stories of Jesus' eating habits, which were startling to many people because he engaged in a countercultural pattern
of eating. Because eating together creates a bond between people,
first-century Jews had many regulations concerning what to eat with
whom. Jesus broke the rules by harvesting on the Sabbath, eating with
public sinners, and sharing vessels with a foreign woman. Although it
is commonplace to eat with one's friends, Jesus turned this practice

upside down: he became friends with the strangers and outsiders with whom he ate. The gospels record that on the last evening before his arrest, Jesus did once more what he had done many times and would do again in a new way after his resurrection: he ate a meal with his followers, sealing a covenant with them around the table.

But this meal was uniquely significant in the community's memory. Although Jesus had created new covenant relationships around the table before, Matthew, Mark, Luke, and Paul all say that at this last supper before his death Jesus established the simple meal of bread and wine as a permanent sign of the covenant between God and the people. The meal made present Christ's death and resurrection, and throughout the ages, his followers would access the benefits of his death and resurrection in their sharing of this meal. The covenant meal sealed a new relationship between God and the people, and in sharing this food, the community around the table became one. The bread is now the body of Christ, which, when shared, forms the assembly into the body of Christ.

The Gospel of John also narrates this last meal before Jesus' death, but in a unique way. John illumines the meaning of the body of Christ by describing the enacted symbol of the footwashing. The new relationship between the members of the body of Christ is to be a covenant of humble service, one to another. If readers of Matthew, Mark, and Luke might imagine the phrase "the body of Christ" in an otherworldly or disembodied way, hazy and indistinct, John places in our hands the actual feet of the next person at table. John's account reminds us that the body of Christ is also the very real people around us, and Jesus tells us to love those people and to wash their feet. The title "Maundy" comes from the Latin word for *command*: Jesus' command that we are to love one another.

Thus according to Matthew, Mark, and Luke, we are to share this meal, and so become the body of Christ, and according to John, we are to wash one another's feet, and so practice the new covenant of love on one another. In the liturgies of the Three Days, the service for Maundy Thursday includes both, telling the story of Jesus' last supper and enacting the footwashing.

Telling the story

The first story told on Maundy Thursday is the account of the Passover from Exodus 12. The angel of death will punish the oppressors, but the blood of the lamb will mark the door of the Israelites, and so God's chosen people will live. For Christians, the blood on our doors that saves us from death is the blood of Christ, shared in the meal at this service, held in mind in the devotion of Good Friday, and celebrated with story and song at the Easter Vigil.

Christians misunderstand their own Holy Week when they think it important to schedule more-or-less Christianized seder meals. When in A.D. 70 the Jerusalem temple was destroyed, the slaughter of the lambs could no longer take place at the temple, and so Jews adapted their Passover ritual to become a solely family festival. At about the same time, Christians were adapting the Passover to focus on Christ's resurrection. The Three Days are the Christian Passover, the ancient nomadic ritual recast by the community that centers its faith now in the transformative power of Christ's death and resurrection. English speakers need to recall that nearly all other Christians call Easter *Pascha*. Because Easter is the Christian Passover, Christians need not conduct seder meals, of which some contemporary Jews might approve and others would be offended, even outraged.

Matthew, Mark, and Luke report that the supper Jesus shared with his followers before his death was a Passover meal. Perhaps it was the kind of festive meal held by a rabbi and his followers. Yet it might be that the evangelists are making a theological point, rather than a historical one. In the Passover meal, the bread reminds the Jews of their years as nomads. Deuteronomy 16 calls the unleavened bread "the bread of affliction," that is, the meal marked by the suffering of their slavery and the difficulties of their escape. For the Christian community, however, the body of Christ is the bread of affliction, and the blood of Christ is the sign of God's new covenant of mercy. Christ bears the sufferings of the people in his body. Now the community's meal of salvation is the bread and wine served up by Christ.

Psalm 116, appointed as the people's response to the first reading, is most appropriate for Maundy Thursday. The psalm passage brings the Jewish Passover into our assembly by speaking of the cup of salvation and the sacrifice of thanksgiving. The psalm also identifies us as God's servants. Freed from our bonds, which brings to mind the exodus, we are freed to serve. Both the Passover meal and the footwashing hover in our minds as we sing the psalm.

The second reading, 1 Corinthians 11:23-26, comes from Paul's reprimand to those first-century Christians who were violating the ideals of community by treating poor people differently from rich people at their communal meals. Paul knows the same history as Matthew, Mark, and Luke: that Jesus established the pattern of this Christian meal on the night that he was betrayed. Paul narrates the last supper in his liturgical instructions to the Corinthians. In our minds, then, added to the story of ancient Israel and its Passover is the account of the Corinthian community proclaiming the Lord's death as they drink and eat the meal. We are like the Israelites fleeing slavery and singing the psalms, and we are also like the Corinthians, learning always how in a fuller way to keep the death of the Lord.

The gospel for Maundy Thursday is John's account of Jesus' last meal with his disciples before his death. Bible readers can count on John's gospel to present always one more layer to the accounts of the ministry of Jesus, to go one step deeper than Matthew, Mark, and Luke. Theologians call this characteristic of John a "higher Christology," that is, that John always describes Jesus as the incarnate God. So it is that in the three-year lectionary, the gospel comes from John on all the most important Christian celebrations: Christmas Day, Maundy Thursday, Good Friday, Easter, and Pentecost, as well as during Lent in year A, and most of Eastertide each year.

Although Matthew, Mark, and Luke say that the last supper was a Passover meal, John's chronology is set one day earlier. According to John, the Passover lambs were being slaughtered while Jesus was on the cross. By this John means to make his point clear: that Jesus is the lamb slain for us. John uses the memory of the last supper to make a different theological point. We need to be prepared for the crucifixion; we need to practice the life of those enlivened by Christ's resurrection. For this reason, Jesus instructs us to wash one another's feet—and of course water always makes Christians think of baptism—readying the entire community for the Passover that is the death and resurrection of Christ. We are to love one another, serving one another in Christ's new covenant of love. So it is that on Maundy Thursday we hear a third story, layered onto those of the exodus and the Corinthian community: we are now the disciples at table, listening to Jesus as he washes our feet.

Enacting the meaning

Throughout the services of the Three Days, we not only hear the story, but we also enact the meaning. The first action scheduled at the service is an amplified rite of confession and forgiveness. This ritual developed out of a practice common during the Middle Ages. Church members who were public sinners or who in some way had scandalized the community had been ostracized during the weeks of Lent, during which time they were supposed to perform some penance that would make up for their sins. These shunned members were received back into the church's fellowship on Maundy Thursday. Hearing John 13, the community practiced Christ's command to love another. Forgiveness was extended to everyone, just in time for them to reenter the full body of the church for the Easter feast. However, this ritual is applicable to us all: we are all sinners, we have all in some way violated the body of Christ, we are all in need of forgiveness. The Maundy Thursday confession and forgiveness may include the laying on of hands with individual absolution for any in the assembly who so desire it.

After the sermon is the footwashing, which has been practiced on this day at least since the seventh century. A hymn from Ghana describes this practice and its meaning:

> Kneels at the feet of his friends,
> silently washes their feet,
> master who pours out himself for them.
>
> Kneel at the feet of our friends,
> silently washing their feet:
> this is the way we will live with you.
>
> Jesu, Jesu,
> fill us with your love,
> show us how to serve
> the neighbors we have from you.
> —Tom Colvin[8]

This footwashing may be organized in a variety of ways. Although in some churches the ordained minister alone washes the feet of twelve people, it is more to John's point that all members of the assembly who wish to participate first have their feet washed, and then in turn kneel before the next person to do the next washing. Children especially can enjoy this ritual, and even toddlers can "help" their parents to dry the wet feet. All you need is pitchers filled with warm water, basins to pour the water into, and piles of towels. In our worship it is not that we are performing a historical passion play, replicating the movements of Jesus. Rather, we are being the church. Enlivened by the Spirit of Christ, we now do what Jesus did: we signify our service to one another in this footwashing.

The classic hymn sung during the footwashing, often known by its Latin title "Ubi caritas," is available in many versions. The text says, "Where there is charity and love, there is God." Not only is God present in the bread and wine, but God is also present in the love symbolized by the ritual of the footwashing. A classic hymn sung during communion on this day, "Thee we adore," was written in about 1260 by Thomas Aquinas, the greatest Christian theologian of the Middle Ages. Some assemblies find it particularly moving to sing a hymn text, perhaps even with the same tune, that Christians have sung for 750 years.

The final action practiced by many assemblies is the stripping of the church. Originally, this practice was simply the utilitarian way to get the altar linens washed once a year. But during medieval times, an elaborate ritual developed in which all the adornments of the sanctuary were removed. Special focus was placed on the stripping of the altar, as if the altar was itself the body of Jesus being stripped before the crucifixion. Currently, most churches have replaced this allegorical understanding of the action with a more psychological emphasis. As one of the lament psalms is sung, we watch as the cross, the books, the candles, the paraments, the linens, any wall hangings, and any extra furniture are removed from the chancel and from around the nave. "You have laid me in the depths of the pit, and darkness is my only companion," says Psalm 88. "Be not far from me, for trouble is near, and there is none to help," says Psalm 22. Finally a bare altar stands naked in an empty chancel in a stripped church. We are being made ready for Good Friday.

A Prayer~

O God, you are our Servant,
kneeling in front of your subjects,
again and again washing us clean.
Train us to serve others
that day by day we may be the body of your Son,
Jesus Christ, our Savior and Lord.
Amen.

For reflection and discussion

1. Do you find the laying on of hands to be an important part of confession and forgiveness on Maundy Thursday? Why or why not?
2. What is your experience with footwashing?
3. What is your opinion about why many congregations do not practice footwashing on Maundy Thursday? (The Amish-Mennonite woman with whom I spoke said, with considerable surprise, "But it's in the Bible!")
4. Is communion more special to you on Maundy Thursday than it is on a Sunday? Why or why not?

4
The Three Days: Good Friday

The tree of life

We call a statement a paradox when it appears to be false, but is shown finally to be true. We first think that a thing is wrong, but by the end we discover that it is right. An example of paradox is the Christian observance of what is called Good Friday. One would think that the day commemorating the execution of a messiah would be kept in unmitigated mourning. Indeed, over the centuries of the church, some Christian communities have dedicated this day to dismal rituals of lament and self-punishment. However, the restored Holy Week rites ask us to keep this good day in a paradoxical way. Our worship is marked not by excessive sorrow, as if we are pretending that Christ is still dead, but rather by solemn devotion. For even on this second of the Three Days we assemble as people of the resurrection. We acknowledge the cross before us as God's gift of life. We wait quietly on this day, the time between the covenant of mercy in the meal and the footwashing and the jubilation at the empty tomb. While we wait, we meditate on the meaning of Christ's cross, and we pray.

Hymnwriter Sylvia Dunstan expresses her faith in this paradoxical nature of Christ in her hymn text, "You, Lord, are both lamb and shepherd." Consider the pairing of images in these two stanzas and refrain:

> You, Lord, are both lamb and shepherd.
> You, Lord, are both prince and slave.
> You, peacemaker and sword-bringer
> of the way you took and gave.
>
> Worthy is our earthly Jesus!
> Worthy is our cosmic Christ!
> Worthy your defeat and victory.
> Worthy still your peace and strife.
>
> You, the everlasting instant;
> you, who are our death and life. [9]

Like the ancient Israelites who saw in the blood on their door the life of the people, Christians mark this day of death as a day that paradoxically brings forth life.

Countless cultures and religious systems have used the image of the cosmic tree to symbolize life for the world, and since the earliest centuries of the church, preachers have used this tree-of-life image to proclaim the paradox of the cross. In Acts (5:30, 10:39, 13:29), the apostles are quoted as referring to the cross as a tree. A sermon delivered in the second century by some unknown preacher includes an extended poetic section on the cross as the tree of life:

> This cross is the tree of my eternal salvation nourishing and delighting me. I take root in its roots, I am extended in its branches. In my tent I am shaded by its shade. Its flowers are my flowers; I am wholly delighted by its fruits. This cross is my nourishment when I am hungry, my fountain when I am thirsty, my covering when I am stripped, for my leaves are no

longer fig leaves but the breath of life. This is the ladder of Jacob, the way of angels. This is my tree, wide as the firmament, which extends from earth to the heavens. It is the pillar of the universe, the support of the whole world. . . . [10]

Much church art has placed side-by-side depictions of the tree of knowledge of good and evil in the Garden of Eden with the tree of death and life on Calvary. It is as if with the eyes of faith, when the church looks at the cross, it sees not an electric chair, but a vibrant tree.

The most famous hymn sung by Christians on Good Friday, called in Latin the *Pange lingua*, celebrates the cross as the tree of life. To tell the story of this hymn, we go back to the fourth century, when Emperor Constantine's mother, Queen Helena, traveled in the Holy Land searching for artifacts from the life of Christ. The story goes that, excavating the hill of Calvary, she found what she believed to be the True Cross. It was this cross that decades later Egeria reverenced in Jerusalem with the kiss ritual.

We now skip a century to discover some fascinating history. In the late fifth century, a Germanic princess named Radegund was kidnapped during battle and reared in a nunnery until at puberty she was to become the fifth wife of Chlotar, the king of the Franks. She was, however, never a willing wife, and finally left her husband to establish a convent in Poitiers, France. Her convent became a great center of learning and devotion. When she heard of an Italian poet whom we call Venantius Fortunatus, she persuaded him to live at her convent as its hymnwriter, and having secured a fragment of the True Cross to be enshrined at her convent, she asked Fortunatus to pen a Holy Week hymn in its honor.

Each year throughout the world Christians sing his hymn, "Sing, my tongue," to celebrate the paradoxical victory of the cross. One stanza is translated in this way:

Faithful cross, true sign of triumph,
Be for all the noblest tree;

> None in foliage, none in blossom,
> None in fruit your equal be;
> Symbol of the world's redemption,
> For your burden makes us free. [11]

Contemporary hymnwriters have continued this tradition. Eric Routley's rendition of a sixteenth-century Hungarian hymn, "There in God's garden," Delores Dufner's "Faithful Cross," and Marty Haugen's "Tree of Life and awesome mystery" exemplify the way that Christians keep Good Friday by seeing a fruitful tree in the wood of the cross.

Telling the story

According to the schedule of biblical readings recommended for use in the ELCA and other Christian denominations, the Sunday that begins Holy Week is a day of contrasts. The entire passion story is proclaimed, Matthew in year A, Mark in year B, and Luke in year C. These accounts tell us of the sufferings of Christ. In Mark, for example, Jesus speaks only once from the cross: a cry of anguish at having been abandoned by God. These synoptic accounts provide a contrast to the joyous palm procession at the beginning of that Sunday's liturgy.

Using the same technique of contrast, the gospel proclaimed on Good Friday is from John. Recall the magisterial details of Christ's passion that appear only in John's gospel. Jesus goes toward the soldiers, knowing all that is to happen to him. Jesus' announcement of himself as the divine I AM causes the troop of soldiers to fall down before him. John refers to the troop as a cohort, which was 600 soldiers. Jesus answers boldly to the high priest, confronts the police, debates with Pilate, and is arrayed in a purple robe. While on the cross, Jesus arranges the future care of his family and followers, and at the moment of his death he gives up his spirit. He is buried with what in our measurement is seventy-five pounds of spices, as only a king would be, and in a garden, a place normally associated with life and growth.

This narration by John proclaims to us that the death of Jesus is, paradoxically, the triumph of Christ as God. As a contrast to the account read from one of the other gospels on Passion Sunday, John's account is the most appropriate reading for Good Friday. John's passion narrative can be proclaimed in various ways: perhaps read aloud by several lectors, perhaps sung in a choral rendition, perhaps chanted by three soloists. In one parish, the pastor read in superb simplicity the entire two chapters of John, and the assembly stood in solemn silence throughout the whole narration. (It was stunning.) John 18–19 is a victorious proclamation of life in the face of death. So if the passion account is read in sections interspersed with congregational hymn singing, care must be taken that the hymns express this same strong picture of the cross as Jesus' throne, rather than as the source of his agony. For example, "Lift high the cross" is far more Johannine than is "Jesus, I will ponder now."

Recently some Christians have hesitated to read the passion from John because of its repeated negative references to "the Jews." Let us face this issue head on. It must first be acknowledged that many times throughout the liturgical year, the language or imagery contained in the Bible readings is alien to our ears and distant from our worldview. This potential to disturb or confuse is one reason why Martin Luther, and many others with him, urged that never would the Bible be read in the assembly without its being explained and expounded in a sermon. In John's passion, for example, the little details—for example, the meaning in Greek of Jesus' answer to the soldiers and their falling down before him—might be missed by hearers unless they had been alerted to the specific meaning of this passage. Perhaps John's gospel above all others requires that we give its text prior attention in Bible study classes and Lenten devotional sessions. John's use of "the Jews" is only the most obvious, and most troubling, of the phrases that call for explication.

Most biblical scholars agree that John's gospel was given its final form in about the year A.D. 95. Antagonism between the Jews who accepted Jesus as messiah and those who did not had increased over the decades, and the evangelist John allows this antagonism to show. Those who opposed the Christian claim that Jesus is the Son of God and Savior of the world, John calls "the Jews." Because also the evangelist was Jewish, and many of the Christian believers at that time were Jews, John's label is clearly a shorthand term expressing the point of view of his Christian community. This labeling by the evangelist did not cause, but did enflame centuries of Christian anti-Semitism.

How ought "the Jews" be translated for contemporary ears? In many passages biblical translators must decide in what ways the English text ought to clarify the meaning of a localized reference or a first-century expression. A simple example is whether our English text should say "the third hour of the day," as does the Revised Standard Version replicating the Greek, or "nine o'clock in the morning," as does the New Revised Standard Version, which is how we say it in English. Some congregations apply this same technique to the Johannine passion account, clarifying the term *the Jews* by translating it as "the Jewish people," "the Jewish authorities," "the Judeans," or "the crowd" in those sentences where such is the meaning. In current speech, the term *the Jews* is always ambiguous, because it can refer to an ethnic designation, a world religion, or many of the inhabitants of a nation-state. This single issue alone suggests that a brief homily on Good Friday is a good idea. Much in these three biblical readings cries out for explication by the contemporary preacher. Even the faithful worshiper needs to hear once again how it is that the death of Christ is recognized as the victory of God, why it is that this day is called good.

The first reading from Isaiah includes several biblical images that Christians use in interpreting the crucifixion of Christ. The prophet describes the coming one as the suffering servant who carries the sorrows of us all by bearing our sins; a vulnerable young plant; the lamb slaughtered in silence; and the warrior, dividing among the people the spoils of victory. In chanting Psalm 22, we join with Jesus on the cross to cry to God in lament. Christ is here seen as the one forsaken by God, a worm, surrounded by a pack of dogs, threatened by a hungry lion, yet the one before whom all the nations shall bow in homage. A passage from the book of Hebrews is next, describing Christ as the Jewish high priest whose mission was to mediate between God and the people. Christ raised up on the cross is like the high priest hovering between the earth and heaven, begging God for divine mercy.

As we attend the cross on Good Friday, the three readings gather together biblical images that help us meditate on the meaning for us of Christ's death. The readings present far more than we can absorb in a single year: Christ as suffering servant, slain lamb, victorious warrior, rejected worm, helpless victim, high priest, incarnate God. It is good if we can come again next year to encounter once more this wealth of images and to contemplate their meaning for us all.

Enacting the meaning

Although Matthew, Mark, and Luke report that most of Jesus' disciples fled, with only the women watching from a distance, John writes that Jesus' mother, several other women and "the disciple whom he loved" stood near the cross. So on Good Friday we join with those faithful few, standing at the foot of the cross. What is the most appropriate action for us to take? We pray.

From the third century on, a central feature of the Good Friday worship has been a lengthy bidding prayer. Taught by Jesus' mother in the story of the wedding at Cana, we come to our Lord pleading, "They have no wine." That is, we pray for other people, bringing to God the needs of everyone we can think of. It is as if in this prayer, we imagine ourselves with the small circle of people at the foot of the cross; but encountering God's love for us, we realize that our circle of care must grow ever wider.

We pray for the church throughout the world, for those who will enter the church in baptism, for the Jewish people, for all those who do not share our faith in Christ, for those who do not believe in God, for those in public office, and finally for all who are in any need. Centered at the cross, we see our arms always expanding to embrace more of the world. Such lengthy praying is a worthy activity on Good Friday and is the model for the intercessory prayer that is part of our communion liturgy each Sunday. Throughout the year, if we find our intercessions becoming too short or too self-focused, we can recall the Good Friday prayer and once again extend our care to encompass more and more of the world.

The Good Friday liturgy presents several other ways for us to enact the meaning of our devotion. Since the fourth century Christians have engaged in some sort of procession of the cross as part of this day's worship. As Egeria describes it, the people processed up to the cross to kiss it in reverence, and some assemblies continue this pattern. In other congregations, it is the cross that processes up the center aisle, with the people meditating on its meaning in their lives. A few churches use an expensive gold or silver cross into which is embedded what is believed to be a fragment of the True Cross. Perhaps the youth group or a carpenter who belongs to the parish constructs a rough-hewn six-foot cross for use in this devotion.

This time of reverence can be kept in many different ways: people may remain in their seats in silent prayer; people may come forward to kneel around the cross; everyone may file by to reverence the cross, perhaps touching it, or making the sign of the cross on their bodies; the choir may sing an appropriate anthem; instrumentalists may offer appropriate meditative music; the congregation may sing Good Friday hymns. Children may bring up dandelions that they have picked and lay them at the foot of the cross. In one New York City congregation, a faithful member was a professional dancer in one of the nation's most renowned dance troupes. Her interpretative dance of lament and transformation before the cross was unforgettable, but best not attempted by amateurs. Perhaps video images of suffering and triumph can be projected, if this presentation can be achieved with technical proficiency.

Using one gesture or another, the assembly enacts its reverence for Christ on the cross. The idea is that the cross that is set up before us stands for the cross on Golgotha, and the cross on Golgotha represents Christ himself. Perhaps all of us own some such symbol, a small thing that comes to represent, even to embody, the great reality behind it. For some married people, their wedding rings are not simply $50 worth of gold. Instead, the rings are practically priceless because they represent the unending circle of their love, and the rings make present every day the blessing that the church gave them on their wedding day. Even a pebble can be granted symbolic power and, for example, can bring onto one's desk the power and beauty of the mountaintop on which it was found. So the cross, accompanied by prayers, music, or art, becomes for us a picture of Christ's cross. Egeria's journey notwithstanding, Christianity did not develop into a religion that requires pilgrimages. In Christianity, Christ is present every Sunday in the local assembly, and a cross that was nailed together by teenage members of the congregation can be for us an image of Calvary itself.

An eighth-century poem written by an unknown Christian in the language of the Anglo-Saxons exemplifies the symbolic way that the cross functions. In "The Dream of the Rood," the poet narrates a vision in which a spectacular tree, hovering in the sky, transmutes itself into the gold processional cross of the church, glittering with gems. But then the visionary sees that the red gems are the glistening blood of Christ, for the cross is "the rood," that is, the wood of the true cross itself. (To translate the Anglo-Saxon word *rood*, think of our word *rod*.) In this poem, the tree itself begins to speak as Christ like a warrior eagerly mounts the cross:

> The young hero stripped himself, he, God almighty,
> strong and stouthearted. He ascended the hated gallows,
> dauntless in the sight of many, to redeem humankind. . . .
> I was raised up a cross; the mighty King I lifted high. [12]

The poem goes on to describe the burial of the cross and finally its exhumation and adornment in silver and gold. Perhaps rather than rubies, we see instead the red spangles that the Sunday school children have glued onto this year's wooden cross.

To accompany Friday's devotion at the cross, some churches use the Solemn Reproaches. Coming to us from the ninth century, this litany imagines God's lament at the manner in which humankind has treated Christ. Each stanza cites first one of God's benevolent gifts and our ungrateful response, and then concludes with the phrase, "and you have prepared a cross for your Savior." The people respond, using an ancient prayer for forgiveness: "Holy God, holy and mighty, holy and immortal, have mercy on us." Because this poem is a complex piece of writing, it would be beneficial to study it before Good Friday so that its meaning will be apparent.

The Three Days are the church's Passover. Repeatedly during the Three Days, we use language from the ancient people of Israel to talk about ourselves. The reproaches follow this pattern. The stanzas recount what God has done for Israel: led it to freedom, fed it with manna, provided water from the rock. But now we in the church use this language in examining ourselves. We have been led to freedom, we have been fed with manna, we have drunk the water from the rock. Yet we have participated in preparing the cross of Christ, and God is reproaching us.

As is possible with a poem in which the meaning is metaphoric and layered, the reproaches came to be misunderstood as a condemnation of the Jews. However, the medieval text of the reproaches has been changed and its intention clarified. The version of the reproaches provided in the worship materials of Lutherans, Methodists, and

Presbyterians makes clear that the poem is the church's accusation of itself.

The current version of this litany is a powerful prayer for mercy. Replete with biblical imagery, it exemplifies the most profound worship pattern that Christians have by applying the Bible's stories of judgment and mercy to ourselves. One musical setting of the current version of the reproaches uses a blues style to convey God's lament.[13] In this way the classic poem is rendered even more readily accessible to our contemporary experience.

The worship service on Good Friday ends with a hymn praising the triumph of the cross. Then the liturgy is merely over, and without a final prayer or blessing the assembly leaves in silence. This practice seeks to make clear that Good Friday is one of the Three Days and that the liturgy continues on Saturday night with the Vigil of Easter. The service feels incomplete, as it ought to. Christians do not remain long on Good Friday, for we are the people of the resurrection.

A Prayer~

O God, you are the Tree of Life,
the blood of your Son its sanguine fruit,
his outstretched arms its mighty branches.
Give us and all the world to eat from this tree,
and by it fix the earth under the heavens
through Jesus Christ, our Savior and Lord.
Amen.

For reflection and discussion

1. What is the way that you prefer the long passion narrative to be proclaimed?

2. Who drafts the intercessions for your assembly each week? Are the prayers full enough of all the needs of the world?

3. What are the possibilities in your assembly, with your talents and granting your heritage, for an appropriate devotion at the procession of the cross?

4. Some popular, perhaps even beloved, depictions of the passion of Christ are criticized as being anti-Semitic. How serious is this issue?

5. What is good, and what is not so good, about the practice of minimal eating on Good Friday?

5
The Three Days: Vigil of Easter

A night different from all other nights

If you have any acquaintance with the Jewish seder meal, you know that the storytelling part of the evening begins with the youngest child asking the question, "Why is this night different from all other nights?" According to ancient Jewish reckoning, a day begins—we would say—the night before. We follow this pattern at Christmastime, when the festivities begin on Christmas Eve. At the seder meal, the Jewish child knows that this particular night of Passover is different from all other nights. The Christian Three Days carries on this ancient tradition by celebrating the great Vigil of Easter at night, on Easter Eve.

It is important to know what the Three Days means by the word *vigil*. Some congregations schedule throughout the year "prayer vigils," at which individuals sign up to pray around the clock in a silent church. Recently some churches schedule just such a prayer vigil all night long on Easter Eve. Perhaps they think of this action as praying at the tomb, waiting for the resurrection. The Easter Vigil of the Three Days is as different from such a ritual as is possible. It offers many readings and actions to the entire assembly, who gather, not to await, but to celebrate the resurrection.

A nighttime meeting of the community is always somewhat extraordinary: only for great events would we gather instead of sleep. The church fathers used the idea of staying awake at the Vigil as a symbol of the Christian lifestyle of waiting for the arrival of God. Furthermore, the recent Christian awareness of ecological issues is well served by several symbols of Easter at night.[14] The sky is dark— perhaps we can see the stars—an apt background for the candlelight of Christ. The service begins with the striking of a fire and the lighting of candles for everyone, a ritual most appropriate for the dark. The moon is full, or close to full, and this cosmological sign of reflected light can function as a sign of our baptismal enlightenment. The ancient notion that the universe was constructed with the four elements of earth, air, fire, and water, is played out in the elements of the Vigil. The very earthiness of the Vigil helps us to see ourselves as creatures of the earth that God created and loves.

Some assemblies, adapting the American Protestant pattern of Easter sunrise services, schedule their Vigil in the wee hours of the morning, beginning the service perhaps an hour and a half before sunrise, about 3:30 A.M., so that when the long liturgy is over, daylight has arrived. Perhaps this pattern will serve your community well. But yet another advantage comes with celebrating Easter in a nighttime Vigil: Easter Day celebrations have the danger of being too facile. The sun is shining, the flowers are blooming, everyone is dolled up in fancy clothes, and so it is easy to sing with gusto about life in the spring. But when we huddle together in the chilly evening, the darkness surrounds us with a sign of death, Christ's death and our own. We are in the tomb of night, and only with faith kindled by the power of the Holy Spirit can we sing of the resurrection. For Easter we meet in the cold dark, just as on Good Friday we read a triumphant gospel: these paradoxes assist us in expressing the depths and heights of the truth of God.

These excerpts from a sermon preached by Asterius, a third-century bishop, illustrate the paradoxes of celebrating resurrection surrounded by darkness:

> O Night brighter than day;
> O Night brighter than the sun;
> O Night whiter than snow;
> O Night more brilliant than torches;
> O Night more delightful than paradise;
> O Night which knows not darkness;
> O Night which has banished sleep;
> O Night which has taught us to join vigil with angels;
> O Night terror of demons;
> O Night most desirable in the year;
> O Night mother of the newly baptized;
> O Night when the devil slept and was stripped;
> O Night in which the Inheritor brought the beneficiaries into
>   their inheritance;
> An inheritance without end.[15]

Perhaps by your standards this preaching is a bit over the top, but at least Asterius does get his point across. The night creates a natural contrast for the celebration of the light of Christ. This night is different from all other nights: it is the night of Christian passover.

At this third of the Three Days, Christians experience together the story of salvation. It is a long story that has continued through the ages, and thus many biblical readings and lots of activities are called for. Perhaps it is not useful to think of the Vigil as "just a bit longer" than a Sunday service. It is a great deal longer, and like an anniversary party that goes on and on into the night, with stories galore and celebrations of various kinds, the Vigil lasts as long as it must, in order to get everything done. What "gets done" is everything the church must do in light of the resurrection: hear the stories of faith, sing the songs of the tradition, baptize the newcomers, share the bread and wine, and so be joined together with Christ as the light of the world.

Telling the story

Anthropologists tell us that many ancient peoples regarded their new year's observance as their most important feast. On that day the elders retold the story of the creation of the world, the establishment of their tribe or the building of their capital city, and with accompanying rituals the community enacted the rebirth of the world. Imagine if, in our society, everyone's birthday was celebrated on the same day: simultaneously everyone's life is renewed. Like these distant tribes, when Christians celebrate our most significant festival, we too tell the story of the creation of the world. Of the several creation stories in the Bible, the one read at the Vigil is Genesis 1, the version that is entirely marked by grace. God created order and beauty out of chaos; the universe is structured to be a good place for its human inhabitants; males and females are created in the divine image; no evil, no sin, no death are yet imagined; and one day in seven is a vacation.

This poem about creation is the first of many readings at the Vigil. We read it not because we are pretending that it is scientifically accurate, but because, like all the readings at the Vigil, it testifies to the faith in God upheld by our tradition, and because it offers us a picture of the resurrection. How can we understand the gospel message of Christ's resurrection? We look to other parts of the Scriptures to see how God brings life out of death. The creation story is one such description of God's gift of life. At this time of God's new creation, at the beginning of our night of storytelling, we tell of God's creative powers at the beginning of time.

In Genesis 1, God begins creation with divine light. (Recall that in this story the sun is not created until the fourth day.) Through the resurrection of Christ, that divine light shines throughout time, and through baptism we bear that illumination in ourselves. For those churches that stress the Vigil as the primary occasion for baptisms, Genesis 1 says that God hovered over primeval waters to create life, and so the church too is birthed from baptismal waters. For Christians who are looking for images of God, for descriptors and metaphors of who and how God is, Genesis 1 shows God as the creator of all, a benevolent mastermind of the universe. (Recall that in the quite different creation story of Genesis 2, the LORD God tries to solve the man's loneliness first with animals, and only later with a woman. In Genesis 1, God knows what to create when.) The Dakota hymn "Many and great, O God, are your works" is a stirring response to Genesis 1. Keep a drumbeat as with the Native Americans of the Midwest you praise the Star-Abiding One.

The other "required reading" at the Vigil is the story from Exodus 14 and 15 of the crossing of the Red Sea. It looks as if the people are doomed: the armed enemy behind them, the impassible sea in front of them, death upon them. In the liturgy, we are those people. Yet God opens a way for us through the sea. Here is yet another picture of the empty tomb: for us, as for the ancient Israelites, God offers a new world. Thanks to the mercy of God, we have escaped from the power of death. The sea serves also as a metaphor for baptism, for we have gone through the waters on our way to the safe side of the sea. Here is also an image of God that can be transformative for those whose God has been too small, only a personal deity. In Exodus, God is the liberator of the oppressed, bringing whole peoples from deathly conditions to a land flowing with milk and honey.

We respond perhaps by singing Miriam's own song: "I will sing to the LORD who has triumphed gloriously." The classic eighth-century hymn by John of Damascus, "Come, you faithful, raise the strain" also applies the imagery of the Exodus to the resurrection community. The chorus of the African American spiritual "O Mary, don't you weep, don't you mourn," holds together the Red Sea and Easter. We sing "O Mary, don't you weep" and think of Mary Magdalene weeping at Jesus' tomb in John 20. Why not weep? "Pharaoh's army got drownded." As we sing, we see the two women singing across the centuries: in fact, the name *Mary* is the Greek form of the Hebrew name *Miriam.* The stories are mirrors of each other, the two women rejoicing in thanks for the life God gives.

If your assembly has the willingness, here is the year's most appropriate occasion for a Miriam to lead a dance. Some congregations have talented dancers who, like a choir, can do for the assembly what it cannot do by itself. Other congregations have experimented with folk dances or conga lines. Yet other assemblies are led in simple hand motions that accompany their song. As we try to remember that worship is not sitting quietly in your pew, this reading may free at least some of us to get out into those aisles and play that tambourine.

The stories of creation and the exodus are the foremost Old Testament readings at the Vigil. Those who want to celebrate the fullest Vigil follow the pattern laid down in the eighth century of twelve Old Testament readings. An entire book could be dedicated simply to these readings, but here we will at least mention each one. For a complete list of the readings for the Vigil of Easter see "Readings for the Three Days" on pages 77–80.

- The tale in Genesis 7–9 of Noah's flood. Almost a second creation story, here God renews the earth, making a new world by washing away the dregs of the old one. As the Welsh poet Ann Griffiths and other Christians say, God is our ark.
- The narrative in Genesis 22 of the testing of Abraham. In this startling, even enigmatic story about moral ambiguity and religious surprise, God saves Isaac from death. Of this story the church fathers said that Christ is our ram.
- The invitation to a feast of salvation from Isaiah 55. God calls us to food, drink, covenant, and the power of the word.
- The call of Woman Wisdom in Proverbs. Divine Wisdom beckons us to walk in her path of justice and share her meal of life.

- The promise in Ezekiel 36 of the new heart and the new spirit that God offers to the community of faith.
- The vision from Ezekiel 37 of the valley of the dry bones. God breathes life back into what is dead. "With the leg bone connected to the knee bone, the knee bone connected to the thigh bone . . . Oh hear the word of the Lord!"
- God's promise of a homeland in Zephaniah 3. God will restore all things to wholeness.
- The legend of Jonah, saved from the sea. In Matthew 12:40, Jesus uses the story of Jonah's three days in the belly of the fish to describe his own death and resurrection.
- Choose either Isaiah or Deuteronomy for yet another example of God's promises of coming life.
- The story in Daniel 3 of the three men in the furnace of blazing fire. God saves the three faithful believers, and in the end even the wicked king gives honor to God.

Each of these readings offers a picture of God's power of resurrection. Each offers us a metaphor for baptism. Each presents us with an image of God. We step into each reading. With the animals we are in the ark, with Abraham we are attempting to obey God, with Isaac we are saved from sacrifice, we are entertained by Woman Wisdom, we are the dry bones enlivened by the breath of God. Finally at our death we are indeed in the furnace of blazing fire, but we have faith in the one who "with the appearance of a god" is with us.

Each of the readings is too good to miss. Read them all, or divide them up over several years. Even the wariest congregation ought to be able to handle seven! Proclaimed superbly, the readings and responses make for an hour, or half an hour, of beloved stories of the faith. Perhaps this part of the Vigil can take place in the church's lounge, with comfortable seats for the adults and a carpet for the children to sprawl on. If you are already in the nave, bring raisins for the kids to snack on. Perhaps the children can bring along to church their favorite stuffed animal, all of us creatures entering the ark once again.

The New Testament reading, Romans 6:3-11, is core Paul. Through our baptism, which we renew at this Vigil, we are joined to the death and resurrection of Christ. We too have died, we too are raised from death, for we are the body of Christ. Perhaps the most appropriate account of the resurrection for the night's gospel proclamation is the one from John. The ELCA's Renewing Worship materials suggest this reading so that the Gospel of John is proclaimed at all three evening services and the other gospels are kept for the Sunday celebrations.[16]

John 20:1-18 presents the most beloved and detailed story of all the evangelists: the disciples find the tomb empty and Mary Magdalene encounters her risen Lord in the garden. It is interesting that in the Greek, Mary calls the gardener *kyrios,* usually translated "Sir." After she has recognized the risen Christ, she tells the disciples that she has seen *kyrios* (same Greek word), usually translated "Lord." By this tradition of translating *kyrios* with its two different meanings, Christians use the narrative of Mary's encounter on Easter to proclaim Christ as both master and as God among us: both human and divine.

Enacting the meaning

At the Vigil, the assembly surrounds the evening of biblical readings with an array of actions. In the course of the liturgy, we do those things that follow from our encounter with the risen Christ: we become lights in the world, we live in our baptism, and we share the bread and wine. Perhaps we also dance! The first of these enactments can be called the fire ceremony of the resurrection, and it begins with the lighting of the new fire.

Still today, the Friday night Sabbath meal of observant Jews begins with the woman of the household lighting the candles on the dinner table. Practically, of course, before electricity, the candles would have to be lit to provide illumination for the meal. But Jews came to see the candle-lighting as symbolic of their faith that in the Sabbath, as at the first day of creation, God brings light into the darkness of our lives. Christians, gathering for evening prayer and lighting the lamps in the room, came to describe the evening light as a sign of Christ, illumining the whole world. The same pattern of practical need turned into symbolic ritual occurs in the Christian observance of Easter.

One story that Christians tell is that when they came to populate the northern areas of Europe, they encountered an annual pagan rite of springtime, in which at a mountainside ceremony, authorized priests struck a new fire to mark the new light of the sun. The people would take home to their hearths coals to enliven their house fire for the next year. The benefits afforded by the fire were seen as coming from the authorities who struck the new fire. The story goes on, that in the seventh century, encountering this ceremony, St. Patrick broke the law by himself striking a grand fire on Ireland's Hill of Slane, proclaiming that the true light of the spring moon was Christ.

The Easter Vigil opens with this same fire. Some anthropologists mark the origins of the creatures we call human beings with the discovery of the uses of fire: a communal center granting light, warmth, protection from predators, and a shared cooked meal. We contemporary Christians join ourselves with the many millennia of assemblies around fire, but we add the words of faith: "The light of Christ." Here is the occasion for a substantial bonfire out-of-doors: we can do better than a cigarette lighter in the narthex.

From the fire the presider lights the paschal candle. Even if our candles are three feet tall, rather than the six-feet-tall man-sized candles of some medieval cathedrals, the candle stands before us as if it were Christ. On Good Friday, the wooden cross represented Christ, and now at the Vigil, the lighted candle is an image of Christ among us. It is marked with a cross and inscribed with the Alpha, the Omega, and the current year's date. In this way the candle proclaims the resurrection of Christ as a timeless event even now occurring. Christ is from the beginning, at the end, and this very year. This night, not back then, is the night of salvation. After the Vigil is completed, the paschal candle will be lighted for the liturgies of the fifty days of Easter, at the font for baptisms, and at the coffin for funerals.

From the paschal candle the fire is spread so that everyone holds a candle. Easter is perhaps the most appropriate time for a candlelight ceremony. As Easter people we think of the story of Pentecost in the book of Acts. No longer is the fire of God only on the top of Mount Sinai; now the fire of God illumines the forehead of each believer. We think also of the lighted candle given to the newly baptized, the fire of the Holy Spirit released in Christ's resurrection. Through baptism, we are all to shine as lights in the world. There under the night sky, and as we process into the building, we remember also the last year's funerals, with the paschal candle burning near the bodies of our loved ones.

Now comes the Easter proclamation. This prayer of blessing from the fourth century makes clear why Christians do not need to attend a Jewish seder. "This is the night," the prayer calls out over and over. For Christians, Easter is the night of the Passover lamb, the escape through the sea, the end of darkness, the rescue from evil, Christ's triumph over hell, even the marriage of heaven and earth. Christ is the Morning Star, the first sign of the coming of day. The prayer praises God for releasing us from the clutches of the sin of Adam. Perhaps the most surprising phrase, one made famous in medieval times, is "O happy fault!" It is as if the sin of humanity is seen to be not only inevitable, but even a good thing, since it brought about the miraculous salvation by Christ.

Longer and shorter versions of this proclamation, called in Latin the Exsultet, the "Rejoice," are available. One of the optional sections of the Easter proclamation is the portion about the bees. God is praised even for the bees, without which we would have no wax for the candle! If you are wondering what bees are doing in this song of praise, you might be interested to hear that even in the fourth century, church leaders debated about these bees. Jerome, the hard-nosed biblical scholar, argued that these nonbiblical critters had no place in the Easter proclamation. But others of the church fathers, like Ambrose and Augustine, promoted this kind of embellished poetic praise. So the bees still buzz around at the close of our Easter proclamation, reminding us of the sweet honey of the word of God.

Some of the medieval manuscripts of the Easter proclamation that have survived the centuries present us with a surprise. The long scrolls are set up with two columns, one of text and one of illustrations. The illustrations depict each of the images presented in the text. The additional surprise is that the illustrations are drawn upside-down: since the scroll hung down over a lectern as the deacon chanted it, the illustrations were meant to be seen, not by the cantor, but by members of the assembly who were sitting close up. So not only in text, but also with illustrations, the Proclamation presented pictures of what Christ's resurrection means for the faithful. Would a video display be our version of an illustrated Exsultet scroll?

The more we reflect on the readings at the Vigil, the majesty of its imagery and the vibrancy of its rituals, the clearer it is that this liturgy is the church's ideal occasion for baptism. Christians of the Middle Ages thought of baptism as the way an infant got saved from hell, and this belief led to baptism being administered privately a few days after birth. However, the church of our time, more like the early church, teaches that baptism inaugurates people into the kingdom of God, enrolls them into the family of believers, and forms them into the body of Christ, and these miracles are effected when the Spirit of God joins us together into the death and resurrection of Christ. Just as the majority of human births occur during the nighttime hours, so the new birth of the baptized can occur at night.

The connection between baptism and Easter is seen not only in the texts of the Vigil, but also in the texts of the rite of baptism. The blessing of the baptismal water praises God for creation and for the exodus—the two foremost Old Testament readings at the Vigil. Thanks to the resurrection of Christ, we have access to God as "the source of all life, the word of salvation, the spirit of mercy."[17] Although many Christians interpret the three dousings of water as a sign of the Trinity, the church fathers taught that the three immersions in the font signified the three days in the tomb. In the water we are buried with Christ and rise with his Spirit to new life.

Whether or not candidates are presented for baptism, the Vigil includes a rite of affirmation of baptism for the entire assembly. Martin Luther spoke about every day of one's Christian life being a return to the font, and at Easter the meaning of that return is celebrated to the fullest. Perhaps the presider uses an evergreen branch to scatter drops of water on the assembly; perhaps each person signs the forehead of another with water from the font. Don't be afraid to get wet: in the water of God is our life.

Finally the assembly enacts the meaning of its baptism and the power of Christ's death and resurrection by sharing in communion. The keeping of this Easter feast is the subject of a famous sermon preached by John Chrysostom in the fourth century:

> Rich and poor together, hold high festival.
> Diligent and heedless, honor this day.
> Both you who have fasted, and you who did not fast,
>   rejoice together today.
> The table is full; all of you, feast sumptuously.
> The calf is fatted; let no one go away hungry.
> Enjoy the feast of faith; receive the riches of God's mercy. [18]

Be sure that the bread is freshly baked and that the wine tastes wonderful and infuses your body with spirit. It's the middle of the night, and we are all hungry to celebrate the resurrection.

Perhaps with a final hymn we can recapitulate all the images of the Vigil. Herbert Brokering's "Alleluia! Jesus is risen"[19] is one such triumphant celebration of Christ's resurrection, as it sings of Christ as the light, the lamb, "heaven forever," the center, the host, our blessing, the vine, the tree, the gift of the future, our clothing, the city, the river of life, and God the I AM. Such superabundance is each Easter "our constant surprise." Truly, the empty tomb is overflowing with the grace of God. The Vigil has lasted two to three hours, perhaps more, and some of us plan to be back in the morning to worship once again. Yet with so plenteous a fare served up at the Vigil, we will be glad to join in this long evening next year, and the next, to eat and eat and eat of the mercy of God.

A Prayer~

O God, you are Life,
Fire in the night,
Honey in the comb,
the Marriage of earth and heaven,
the new Creation,
Pathway across the sea,
Flesh on dead bones,
Water on parched earth,
Bread and Wine for a hungry world.
Give us your Spirit of life,
life as of the empty tomb of your Son,
Jesus Christ, our Savior and Lord.
Amen.

For reflection and discussion

1. Are you concerned about any potential hazards of the bonfire and individual candles? Why or why not?
2. Which is your favorite Old Testament reading? Why?
3. What is the best way in your situation to use liturgical dance?
4. How much water does your assembly use in baptism? Three drops? Three scoops? Three bucketfuls? Three submersions?
5. How can you serve up the bread and wine so that it is recognized as the food of God and the feast of life?
6. What is the best time of night for your congregation to schedule this Vigil?

6
The Three Days: Easter Sunday

On this day

Perhaps you recognize these words of praise:

> It is indeed right, our duty and our joy,
> that we should at all times and in all places
> give thanks and praise to you, almighty and merciful God,
> through our Savior Jesus Christ;
> who on this day overcame death and the grave,
> and by his glorious resurrection
> opened to us the way of everlasting life.

This sentence serves as the beginning of the presiding minister's prayer of thanksgiving over the bread and wine at the Sunday liturgy: that is, at every Sunday liturgy. It is not the more elaborate initial thanksgiving appointed especially for Easter Day, but instead is the standard praise for every nonfestival Sunday. Every Sunday is a celebration of the Resurrection of Our Lord.[20] Christians meet on Sunday because "on this day," as the prayer states, Christ rose from the dead. Perhaps it is the first Sunday of September or the last Sunday of January, but if we have assembled on a Sunday, Christ arose "on this day."

So it is that the morning service on Easter Day need not be thought of as the sole annual celebration of the resurrection. Of course exuberant music and festive flowers are appropriate. But music and flowers are appropriate on most Sundays, because every Sunday is the new creation, the day of feasting with the risen Lord, and the renewal of the community's life in the Spirit of Christ. Although the Sunday of the Resurrection of Our Lord can have special focus and particular celebration, it is upheld by the fifty days of Easter and surrounded by a full year's worth of festive Sunday meals. Easter Day need not go it alone.

Moreover, it is perhaps painful to realize that at least for the countless people who come to church only at Easter, both the choirs and the flowers of a stereotypical Easter service are somewhat nonparticipatory presentations. The insiders of the parish offer an elaborate event, more musical instrumentation than usual, more potted flowers than usual. From the pew the people listen to the music and look at the flowers. Such a service may be magnificent in how it tells the story of the resurrection, but it offers far less to the entire assembly than did the Vigil in enacting the meaning of the resurrection.

But people always seek ways to enact meaning. Recall that from the fifth and sixth centuries on, the Three Days had fallen into disuse. By the ninth century the full Three Days of liturgies were held nearly nowhere. Yet the people of God wanted to enact the resurrection. To fill this void, especially in the monasteries at their daily prayer, the biblical conversation between the angel and the women at the tomb developed into mini-plays. This dialogue is known by its Latin beginning, "Quem quaeritis" (whom do you seek?). Taking the part of the angel, half of the monastery choir would sing, "Whom do you seek in the tomb?" The other half, echoing the women at the tomb, would answer, "Jesus of Nazareth, who was crucified." The first group would respond, "He is not here; he is risen."

A tenth-century English bishop wrote out directions for this small play. According to his instructions, the monk who played the angel was to wear an alb and hold a palm branch, and the monks who played the three Marys were to wear copes and carry censors. The "three Marys" concluded the presentation by singing,

> Alleluia! The Lord is risen today,
> The strong lion, the Christ, the Son of God.
> Give thanks to God! Sing Alleluia! [21]

Calling Christ "the strong lion" hints at the direction that these chancel dramas were headed. By the twelfth century, the dramatizations had become more and more fanciful and less and less biblical, and church leaders removed them from the liturgy and sent them out into the streets. From this developed the medieval mystery plays. Performed by town guilds, the plays came to be embellished in quite nonbiblical ways for the entertainment of the audiences. Thus there is nothing new about church leaders criticizing popular dramatizations of the life of Christ as playing loose with the biblical text and being infused with questionable theology and fabricated nonsense.

In the twentieth century, before the revival of the Three Days, Protestants once again felt the need to create a special service for Easter. Inspired both by the Moravians of North Carolina and by an evangelical Protestant pastor in Colorado, churches began to hold Easter sunrise services. The Colorado version, which drew thousands of worshipers and was broadcast by radio throughout the country, meant to replicate the narrative in John 20 by situating the service in a garden. The Colorado "garden" was a stunning landscape famous for its red sandstone rock formations.

Sometimes the idea undergirding such worship is to return us to biblical times, to bring us back to the garden John describes, to gather precisely at dawn for the moment of Christ's resurrection. The liturgies of the Three Days, however, imply a different understanding of liturgy. Throughout the Three Days, we are not becoming biblical people in their time and place. Rather, we are becoming more and more our baptized selves. We are practicing what it means to be the body of Christ here and now. On Easter we celebrate the resurrection of Christ, which is always recognized as a present event. Easter is "on this day," and it calls us, not toward the past, but into God's future.

The task in our time for Easter Day is to design a superb simple Sunday service. It is hoped that each year a larger and larger percentage of the congregation will have joined together in the liturgies of the Three Days. Thus they will already have participated in a many-faceted, several-hours-long celebration of Easter, gone home to eat some chocolates and sleep a little, and come back once again the next morning, assembling for the different kind of Easter celebration that daylight affords. The sun makes of this liturgy something other than did the darkness and candles of the liturgy the night before.

An important emphasis for our Easter Day celebrations is the Christian understanding that God's gifts will come fully only finally at the end of time. Although God's presence is always "now," it is also "not yet." Today is not the final resurrection; we look toward the conclusion of the story of the body of Christ. Our plenteous festivities must open toward the future so that we want what God has still to bring to the world. The splendor of our liturgy ought never suggest that we have already arrived.

Telling the story

The first reading, Acts 10:34-43, is an Easter sermon ascribed to Peter. The final verses of Peter's address speak of God's judgment and God's forgiveness. Once again we encounter the two sides of the biblical message: both justice and mercy characterize our God. The psalm response, Psalm 118, recalls the reading the night before about Israel crossing the Red Sea, for now we are the people dancing in joy at God's victory over evil. It is "on this day" that the LORD has acted, we sing (Ps. 118:24).

We build upon the once-rejected stone, and so we think of the stone rolled away from the empty tomb. In the second reading from Colossians or 1 Corinthians we hear the early Christians acclaim their faith in the resurrection and its meaning in their lives. All the readings resonate with our memories of last evening's actions.

If John's resurrection account was read at the Vigil, Sunday morning's service will return to Matthew's account in year A, Mark's in year B, and Luke's in year C. Recall that Matthew, Mark, or Luke's passion narrative was proclaimed on Passion Sunday and John's passion narrative was read on Good Friday. Following this same pattern, the assembly hears two different biblical accounts of the resurrection, one at the Vigil and one on Sunday morning. Each gospel tells the story differently. The contrast between two accounts is most startling in year B, when next to John's beloved narration of the encounter between Mary Magdalene and the risen Christ in the garden, we hear this closing sentence from Mark: that the women "went out and fled from the tomb, for terror and amazement had seized them; and they said nothing to anyone, for they were afraid" (Mark 16:8). What a task it is to preach on Mark's Easter gospel!

Enacting the meaning

Every Sunday, but especially on Easter, the assembly enacts the message of salvation by sharing in the bread and wine of communion. The body of Christ has risen from the dead, and enlivened by the Spirit of the risen Christ, we share in that body and so become that body. As the phrase goes, we are what we eat. Easter is our foremost day of thanksgiving, which is what is meant by the ancient Greek name for the communion service, *eucharist*.

Perhaps of the hymns that are sung, each one can come from a different time and place, so that we join with Christians of the sixth, the twelfth, the sixteenth, the eighteenth, the nineteenth, and the twentieth centuries, from Europe and Africa and the Americas, to laud the resurrection. Perhaps before the service begins, the assembly can join in a sing-along so that even more hymns, both those dearly beloved and those newly composed, can help us enact the meaning of the day. It may be that a sing-along can more fully engage the whole assembly in the meaning of Easter than can their listening to anthems by several choirs.

Perhaps on Easter Day the intercessions can be particularly full of the needs of the earth and the woes of the world's peoples: we are quite aware of countless sufferers whose Easter is marked by pain and privation, rather than celebration and plenty. Perhaps the contributions from the gathering of the gifts can be dedicated to a local charity, rather than to parish maintenance, so that the assembly can in that small way be the witnesses that Peter describes (Acts 10:39). Perhaps the service will conclude with a full rite of the sending of the communion ministers. As they are commissioned to carry the bread and wine to those who are homebound, they might also hold up one of the flowering plants, taking some of the beauty of the service to those who were absent. Perhaps the most appropriate dismissal sentence on Easter Day is the newly proposed "Go in peace. Share the good news." We are now the women running from the tomb, living in a new way because we are now that risen body of Christ.

The Three Days all year

We have thought of the Three Days as a feast. Similarly, we can think of the three years of the lectionary as a banquet. Indeed, Sunday after Sunday is modeled on the Three Days. Each week we remember our baptism into Christ's death and resurrection. Each week we read from the Old Testament, the epistles, and the gospels. Each week we share in the bread and wine. Throughout the year, biblical readings that speak of our servanthood bring to mind the footwashing of Maundy Thursday. Each Sunday when we offer intercessions, we recall the all-embracing bidding prayer of Good Friday. Whenever our culture or a world religion puts before us the image of the tree of life, we remember reverencing the cross. When we pass candlelight around the nave on Christmas Eve, we think not only of, perhaps, the stars over Bethlehem, but also of the baptismal light of Christ at Easter.

Echoes of the Easter Vigil readings sound throughout the three years of our Sunday lectionary. On the fifth Sunday in Lent in year A, for example, we hear the rattle of Ezekiel's dry bones. On the first Sunday in Lent in year B we listen to the conclusion of the story of Noah and the flood. On Trinity Sunday in year A we hear the creation story from Genesis 1. During the year B summertime reading of John's Bread of life discourse we again hear the call of Proverb's Woman Wisdom. Several times through the three years we hear the invitation from Isaiah 55. At each of these services the Three Days calls out to us: Christ has died and is risen for us.

We go from one Three Days feast to the next, tasting its food in little ways throughout the year. During the Three Days we have filled our worship with activities. We have stood and processed and knelt, eaten and drunk, sung and kept deep silence, washed feet, touched a cross, lighted a bonfire, held a candle, gotten wet, and danced at the sea. Because of these activities, we may be freer to enrich our telling of the story by enacting its meaning all the other Sundays of the year. Because for the Three Days we found ways to involve our members of all ages in worship, we might be inspired to keep up this inclusion Sunday after Sunday.

One final Lutheran word

This small book hopes to provide inspiration and encouragement as assemblies revive the full liturgies of the Three Days and each year mature more deeply into them. Of course these services, like any others, can be poorly planned and sloppily executed, with little preparation and minimal participation provided for the assembly. But it would take excessive thoughtlessness, considerable ignorance, and massive negligence to diminish the significance of the footwashing, the procession of the cross, the lighting of the paschal candle, the reading of our most compelling biblical stories, the baptisms and the first eucharist of Easter, all supported by two thousand years' worth of hymns. On the other hand, planning for full participation in all of the readings and actions of the Three Days can become an impetus for the renewing of all the assembly's worship.

Our care for excellent liturgy, however, even our accomplishment of a magnificent Three Days feast, will not save the world. Martin Luther reminds us never to claim too much for the church's worship. Our faith, instead, is that God will save the world. Luther's Easter hymn "Christ Jesus lay in death's strong bands" magnificently summarizes all the emphases of the Three Days.

> Here the true Paschal Lamb we see,
> Whom God so freely gave us;
> He died on the accursed tree—
> So strong his love—to save us.
> See, his blood now marks our door;
> Faith points to it; death passes o'er. . . .
>
> So let us keep the festival
> To which the Lord invites us;
> Christ is himself the joy of all,
> The sun that warms and lights us. . . .
>
> Then let us feast this Easter Day
> On Christ, the bread of heaven. . . .
> Christ alone our souls will feed;
> He is our meat and drink indeed;
> Faith lives upon no other! Hallelujah![22]

Our hope for the renewal of all things rests not in our more-or-less successful worship, but in God.

Such a salvation deserves our best attempts at praise and proclamation. As we say in a beloved Lutheran eucharistic prayer, "We give thanks to you, Lord God Almighty, not as we ought, but as we are able."[23] I hope you come to agree with me that the Three Days will enable the church's assemblies more profoundly and with more participation to tell the story and to enact the meaning of the death and resurrection of Christ.

Come to the feast!

A Prayer~

O God, week after week you arise,
gathering your people,
proclaiming your word of life,
feeding us with food that is eternal,
sharing your Spirit,
and renewing the face of the earth.
O God, transform us by this resurrection,
that we may embrace all that you have made
and live toward the justice that you intend
through Jesus Christ, our Savior and Lord.
Amen.

For reflection and discussion

1. What is good, and what is not so good, about a more modest Easter Day service?

2. What would you preach on the years that the resurrection account from the Gospel of Mark is proclaimed?

3. What is your opinion about scheduling an Easter egg hunt after worship on Easter Day?

4. Have you heard of churches at which the Easter Bunny shows up for worship? What do you think about this practice?

5. Which suggestion for worship made in this book did you find most helpful? Which did you think was most bizarre?

Readings
for The Three Days

Maundy Thursday

A, B, C

Exodus 12:1-4 (5-10) 11-14   *The passover of the LORD*
Psalm 116:1-2, 12-19   *I will take up the cup of salvation and call on the
    name of the LORD. (Ps. 116:13)*
1 Corinthians 11:23-26   *Proclaim the Lord's death until he comes*
John 13:1-17, 31b-35   *The service of Christ: footwashing and meal*

Good Friday

A, B, C

Isaiah 52:13—53:12   *The suffering servant*
Psalm 22   *My God, my God, why have you forsaken me? (Ps. 22:1)*
Hebrews 10:16-25   *The way to God is opened by Jesus' death*
or Hebrews 4:14-16; 5:7-9   *Jesus is our merciful high priest*
John 18:1—19:42   *The passion and death of Christ*

Resurrection of Our Lord, Vigil of Easter

A, B, C (Old Testament readings)

1

Genesis 1:1—2:4a   *Creation*

2

Genesis 7:1-5, 11-18; 8:6-18; 9:8-13   *Flood*

3

Genesis 22:1-18   *Testing of Abraham*

4

Exodus 14:10-31; 15:20-21   *Deliverance at the Red Sea*

5

Isaiah 55:1-11   *Salvation freely offered to all*

6

Proverbs 8:1-8, 19-21; 9:4b-6   *The wisdom of God*
or Baruch 3:9-15, 32—4:4   *The wisdom of God*

7

Ezekiel 36:24-28   *A new heart and a new spirit*

8

Ezekiel 37:1-14   *Valley of the dry bones*

9

Zephaniah 3:14-20   *Gathering of God's people*

10

Jonah 1:1—2:1   *Call of Jonah*
or Jonah 3:1-10   *Call of Jonah*

11

Isaiah 61:1-4, 9-11   *Clothed in the garments of salvation*
or Deuteronomy 31:19-30   *The song of Moses*

12
Daniel 3:1-29   *Deliverance from the fiery furnace*

A, B, C (New Testament readings)
Romans 6:3-11   *Dying and rising with Christ*
John 20:1-18   *Seeing the risen Christ*

Resurrection of Our Lord, Easter Day

A

Acts 10:34-43   *God raised Jesus on the third day*
or Jeremiah 31:1-6   *Joy at the restoration of God's people*
Psalm 118:1-2, 14-24   *This is the day that the LORD has made; let us rejoice and be glad in it. (Ps. 118:24)*
Colossians 3:1-4   *Raised with Christ to seek the higher things*
or Acts 10:34-43   *God raised Jesus on the third day*
Matthew 28:1-10   *Proclaim the resurrection*
or John 20:1-18   *Seeing the risen Christ*

B

Acts 10:34-43   *God raised Jesus on the third day*
or Isaiah 25:6-9   *The feast of victory*
Psalm 118:1-2, 14-24   *This is the day that the LORD has made; let us rejoice and be glad in it. (Ps. 118:24)*
1 Corinthians 15:1-11   *Witnesses to the risen Christ*
or Acts 10:34-43   *God raised Jesus on the third day*
Mark 16:1-8   *Empty tomb, announcement of the resurrection*
or John 20:1-18   *Seeing the risen Christ*

C

Acts 10:34-43   *God raised Jesus on the third day*
or Isaiah 65:17-25   *God promises a new heaven and a new earth*
Psalm 118:1-2, 14-24   *This is the day that the LORD has made; let us rejoice and be glad in it. (Ps. 118:24)*

1 Corinthians 15:19-26   *Christ raised from the dead, the first fruits*
or Acts 10:34-43   *God raised Jesus on the third day*
Luke 24:1-12   *The women proclaim the resurrection*
or John 20:1-18   *Seeing the risen Christ*

Acknowledgments

Excerpts from the following sources are gratefully acknowledged:

Page 15: *Egeria: Diary of a Pilgrimage,* from Ancient Christian Writers, no. 38, translated and annoted by George E. Gingras, Ph.D. Copyright © 1970 Rev. Johannes Quasten, Rev. Walter J. Burghardt, SJ, Thomas Comerford Lawler, and The Newman Press, N.Y./Mahway, N.J. Used with permission of Paulist Press. www.paulistpress.com

Pages 23-24: *On Pascha* by Melito of Sardis, tr. Stuart George Hall, tr. © 1979 S. G. Hall. Used by permission.

Page 29: "Holy God, holy and glorious" by Susan Briehl. Copyright © 2000 GIA Publications, Inc. Used by permission.

Page 38: "Jesu, Jesu, fill us with your love," words by Tom Colvin. Copyright © 1969 Hope Publishing Co., Carol Stream, IL 60188. All rights reserved. Used by permission.

Page 42: "You, Lord, are both lamb and shepherd," by Sylvia Dunstan. Copyright © 1991 GIA Publications, Inc. Used by permission.

Pages 42-43, 55: *The Paschal Mystery,* tr. Thomas Halton. Copyright © 1969 Society of St. Paul, Alba House.

Page 50: "When the Cross Tells the Story" in *Liturgy,* trans. Gail

Notes

Chapter one

1. *Egeria: Diary of a Pilgrimage*, tr. and ed. George E. Gingras, vol. 38 of *Ancient Christian Writers* (New York: Paulist Press, 1970), 111.

Chapter two

2. *The Journals of Henry Melchior Muhlenberg*, tr. Theodore G. Tappert and John W. Doberstein (Philadelphia: Muhlenberg Press, 1958), III:737. See also II:217.

3. For a simplified description of these ceremonies see Stan Padilla, *Deer Dancer: Yaqui Legends of Life* (Summertown, TN: Book Publishing Company, 1998).

4. Interview with Ada Fischer, Beachy Amish-Mennonite, in Lancaster, Pennsylvania, July 19, 2004. The Beachy Amish-Mennonites are not as conservative as the Old Order Amish.

5. Melito of Sardis, *On Pascha*, tr. Stuart George Hall (Oxford: Clarendon Press, 1979), 59.

6. Susan Palo Cherwien, "Bright Joining: Meditations on the Cross" in *O Blessed Spring: Hymns of Susan Palo Cherwien* (Minneapolis: Augsburg Fortress, 1997), 15.

7. Susan R. Briehl, "Holy God, Holy and Glorious," in *New Hymns and Songs,* Renewing Worship, vol. 5 (Minneapolis: Augsburg Fortress, 2003), R201.

Chapter three
8. Tom Colvin, "Jesu, Jesu, Fill Us with Your Love," in *With One Voice* (Minneapolis: Augsburg Fortress, 1995), 765.

Chapter four
9. Sylvia Dunstan, "You, Lord, Are Both Lamb and Shepherd," in *Voices United* (Etobicoke, Ontario: The United Church Publishing House, 1996), 210.

10. Anonymous, "The Pasch History," in *The Paschal Mystery: Ancient Liturgies and Patristic Texts*, ed. A. Hamman (Staten Island, NY: Alba House, 1969), 64–65.

11. Venantius Honorius Fortunatus, "Sing, My Tongue," in *Lutheran Book of Worship* (Minneapolis: Augsburg Publishing House and Philadelphia: Board of Publication, Lutheran Church in America, 1978), 118.

12. Translation by Gail Ramshaw, "When the Cross Tells the Story," in *Liturgy* 1:1 (1980), 10–13. Also available in *The Earliest English Poems*, tr. Michael Alexander (New York: Penguin Books, 1966), 103–110.

13. Robert Buckley Farlee, "Solemn Reproaches of the Cross," Minneapolis: Augsburg Fortress, 2001.

Chapter five
14. See Benjamin M. Stewart, "A Tree Planted by Water: Ecological Orientation at the Vigil of Easter," S.T.M. thesis, Lutheran Theological Seminary at Philadelphia, 2004; and Anscar J. Chupungco, O.S.B., *Shaping the Easter Feast* (Washington, DC: Pastoral Press, 1992).

15. Asterius of Amasea, "Homily 19," in *The Paschal Mystery: Ancient Liturgies and Patristic Texts*, ed. A. Hamman (Staten Island, NY: Alba House, 1969), 109–110.

16. See *The Church's Year,* Renewing Worship, vol. 8 (Minneapolis: Augsburg Fortress, 2004) 99–108, 266.

17. See *Holy Baptism and Related Rites*, Renewing Worship, vol. 3 (Minneapolis: Augsburg Fortress, 2002), 9.

18. John Chrysostom, "Easter Homily," in Gabe Huck, *The Three Days: Parish Prayer in the Paschal Triduum* (Chicago: Liturgy Training Publications, 1981), 80.

19. Herbert F. Brokering, "Alleluia! Jesus Is Risen," in *With One Voice* (Minneapolis: Augsburg Fortress, 1995), 674.

Chapter six

20. For a discussion of every Sunday as Easter, see Gail Ramshaw, *A Three-Year Banquet* (Minneapolis: Augsburg Fortress, 2004), 27.

21. "Quem quaeritis," http://www.northern.edu/wild/th100/quem.htm.

22. Martin Luther, "Christ Jesus Lay in Death's Strong Bands," in *Lutheran Book of Worship* (Minneapolis: Augsburg Publishing House and Philadelphia: Board of Publication, Lutheran Church in America, 1978), 134.

23. *Lutheran Book of Worship* Ministers Desk Edition (Minneapolis: Augsburg Publishing House and Philadelphia: Board of Publication, Lutheran Church in America, 1978), 225. See also *Holy Communion and Related Rites*, Renewing Worship, vol. 6 (Minneapolis: Augsburg Fortress, 2004), 15.

Bibliography

Adam, Adolf. *The Liturgical Year: Its History and Its Meaning After the Reform of the Liturgy.* Tr. Matthew J. O'Connell. New York: Pueblo, 1981. Explicates the post-Vatican II rites of the Roman Catholic Church.

Chupungco, Anscar J., O.S.B. *Shaping the Easter Feast.* Washington, DC: Pastoral Press, 1992. Discusses how the elements of nature functioned during the early centuries of the church's Easter celebration.

Davies, J. G. *Holy Week: A Short History.* Richmond: John Knox Press, 1963. Compact history of the week's liturgies.

Hickman, Hoyt L., et al. "From Ashes to Fire: Lent and Easter/Pentecost," in *The New Handbook of the Christian Year.* Nashville: Abingdon, 1992. Explicates the rites as published by the United Methodist Church.

Huck, Gabe. *The Three Days: Parish Prayer in the Paschal Triduum.* Chicago: Liturgy Training Publications, 1981. Detailed suggestions for keeping the Three Days at home and in the parish.

Ramshaw, Gail. *Words around the Fire.* Chicago: Liturgy Training Publications, 1990. Meditations and prayers based on seven of the Easter Vigil readings.

This Is the Night. Chicago: Liturgy Training Publications, 1992. A video presentation of a Roman Catholic parish in Texas preparing for and celebrating baptisms at the Vigil.

A Triduum Sourcebook. Ed. Gabe Huck and Mary Ann Simcoe. Chicago: Liturgy Training Publications, 1983. Collection of quotations from Christian history pertinent to keeping the Three Days.

Notes on the Three Days

Notes on the Three Days

Notes on the Three Days

OTHER Worship Matters TITLES

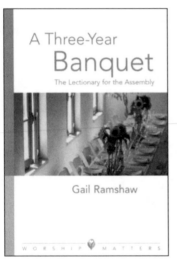

A Three-Year Banquet: The Lectionary for the Assembly
by Gail Ramshaw

A Three-Year Banquet invites the entire worshiping assembly, lay and clergy, to understand and delight in the three-year lectionary. The study guide explains how the Revised Common Lectionary was developed and how the gospels, the first readings, and the epistles are assigned. Further chapters describe many ways that the three readings affect the assembly's worship and the assembly itself. Like food at a banquet, the fare we enjoy in the lectionary nourishes us year after year.

0-8066-5105-9

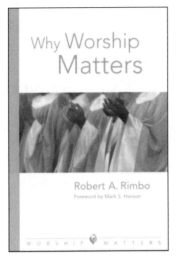

Why Worship Matters
by Robert A. Rimbo
Foreword by
Mark S. Hanson

Why Worship Matters is the first volume in a series centering on the Renewing Worship project of the Evangelical Lutheran Church in America. This little volume is a conversation-starter for those who want to look at the assembly's worship in very broad terms. It also invites reflection on the needs of the world, individuals, the church, and society in light of the assembly's central activity, worshiping God.

08066-5108-3

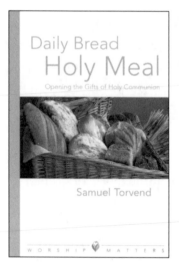

Daily Bread, Holy Meal: Opening the Gifts of Holy Communion
by Samuel Torvend

Daily Bread, Holy Meal invites Christians to reconsider the significance of eating and drinking with Jesus of Nazareth in a world of great need. Drawing on recent biblical and historical studies, this exploration of the Eucharist asks the seeker in every Christian to consider the ecological, theological, communal, and ethical dimensions of the Lord's supper. Through a careful weaving of biblical passages, medieval poetry, Luther's writings, familiar hymns, and newly-written liturgical texts, each chapter unfolds another "gift" of the Holy Communion and the sometimes troubling questions each one raises for individuals who live in a fast food culture yet seek community around a gracious table.

0-8066-5106-7

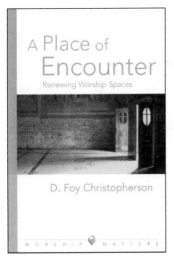

A Place of Encounter: Renewing Worship Spaces
by D. Foy Christopherson

House, temple, theatre, warehouse, courtroom, auditorium, TV studio, or lecture hall? River or baptistery or pool? Dining room or catacomb? House of God or house of the church? In its 2000-year history the church has tried on many buildings, and is ever seeking a more comfortable skin. Exactly what that skin will look like is guided by how the church understands itself, by how it worships, and by what it understands its mission to be. *A Place of Encounter* brings clarity and insight to congregations and individuals who are interested in exploring how our worship spaces serve, form, and proclaim.

0-8066-5107-5

The Three-Day

Feast

Maundy Thursday, Good Friday, Easter

The restoration of the Three Days at the heart of the church's year remains one of the great projects in the ongoing renewal of congregational life and mission. In rich and vivid detail, Gail Ramshaw shows us how the ancient and ever new Easter feast both tells the story of God's mercy in Jesus' death and resurrection and enacts its meaning for our lives, for this world. This book will inform, inspire, and delight all who seek to keep these days.

—Thomas H. Schattauer
Professor of Liturgics and Dean of the Chapel
Wartburg Theological Seminary, Dubuque, Iowa

In her short book *The Three-Day Feast*, Gail Ramshaw draws us across this globe and through time into the varied and rich traditions of the church for Maundy Thursday, Good Friday, and Easter. In so doing she awakens our hunger and longing for the three-day feast as we hunger for the bread and wine and for Christ himself. I love this book.

—April Ulring Larson
Bishop, La Crosse Area Synod
Evangelical Lutheran Church in America

Gail Ramshaw, a Lutheran laywoman, is a scholar of liturgical language. She is the author of many liturgical resources, including *Treasures Old and New: Images in the Lectionary* and *A Three-Year Banquet: The Lectionary for the Assembly*. She served on the Renewing Worship development panel for *The Church's Year: Propers and Seasonal Rites*, Renewing Worship, vol. 8.

Augsburg Fortress
www.augsburgfortress.org

ISBN 080665115-6

9 780806 651156

9 0 0 0 0

W O R S H I P
M A T T E R S
Viewpoints on renewing our worship